"With a mixture of historical scholarship and careful critical reading, Graham Holderness makes a very powerful case for seeing Shakespeare as a committed and self-conscious Protestant in his mature works. This crisp and lively book will challenge a number of popular orthodoxies and will stimulate some fresh readings of the major plays; it makes it harder than ever to think of Shakespeare as indifferent to the great questions of faith."

Dr Rowan Williams, academic and theologian

"Shakespeare's faith was part of his project as a playwright. Graham Holderness's illuminating account presents Shakespeare as an imaginatively engaged Calvinist of his age, bodying forth on stage a world in which divine will can at best only be hoped for, and for which it is worth risking everything."

Paul Edmondson, The Shakespeare Birthplace Trust, and author of *Shakespeare: Ideas in Profile*

"This book is informative, engaging, and forthright in its argument. Contextualizing Shakespeare historically, Graham Holderness offers careful and incisive readings of a wide range of plays, urging that the playwright's faith is not only discernible but also important to our understanding of Shakespeare's extraordinary achievement."

John D. Cox, DuMez Professor of English Emeritus, Hope College

"The Bible *and the* Book of Common Prayer *saturate the plays of Shakespeare, yet his religion is elusive and debated. Graham Holderness's book places the bard in the very centre of the English Reformation and the emergent Anglican tradition. This is a study that everyone seriously concerned to understand Shakespeare should read."*

Revd Professor David Jasper, Professor of Literature and Theology, University of Glasgow

"*This is a timely and helpful book. After decades of wilful secularism, Shakespeare criticism has recently taken a 'religious turn' and fresh work is being done to show the depth and subtlety of the Christian faith that undergirds the plays. Likewise recent work in theology has emphasized the importance of the poetic imagination in our approach to the mystery of faith. Graham Holderness offers a deeply informed and well balanced account both of the Christian context of Shakespeare's plays, and more importantly of their Christian content. The debate over Shakespeare's personal church allegiance will continue, but* The Faith of William Shakespeare *illuminates a faith that itself illuminates and is illuminated by the plays. Readers will finish this book with a richer understanding not only of the plays and the period, but of the Christian faith itself.*"

Malcolm Guite, poet, theologian and chaplain of Girton College

THE FAITH
OF WILLIAM
SHAKESPEARE

Graham Holderness

LION

Published by Lion Books
an imprint of
Lion Hudson plc
Wilkinson House, Jordan Hill Road,
Oxford OX2 8DR, England
www.lionhudson.com/lion

ISBN 978 0 7459 6891 9
e-ISBN 978 0 7459 6892 6

First edition 2016

A catalogue record for this book is available from the British Library

Printed and bound in the UK, October 2016, LH26

Contents

In memory of my brother Stephen
1963 – 2016
Whom we love, but see no longer.

ACKNOWLEDGMENTS

All quotations from Shakespeare, including act, scene, and line references, are from *The Norton Shakespeare: Based on the Oxford Edition*, edited by Stephen Greenblatt, Walter Cohen, Jean E. Howard, and Katharine Eisaman Maus (New York and London: W. W. Norton, 1997). Quotations from the Bible, with book, chapter and verse, are from the Geneva Bible, first published 1557–60 but first published in England as a complete Bible in 1576. Quotations from *The Book of Common Prayer* are taken from the 1559 edition, and the quotations from the "Thirty-nine Articles" from the 1662 edition of *The Book of Common Prayer*. Quotations from John Calvin's *Institutes of the Christian Religion* are taken from the translation by Henry Beveridge (1845).

PREFACE

William Shakespeare was a Christian. He was baptized, married, and buried in the Church of England. In his dramatic works he drew extensively on the English Bible and on *The Book of Common Prayer*. The world views that emerge from his plays lie firmly within the Christian universe of sixteenth-century Europe, except when he was reconstructing pre-Christian societies such as those of Ancient Greece or Rome. Notwithstanding the familiar claims that his work is universally valuable and of permanent significance (claims which continue to be made by proponents of the present as a secular, "post-Christian" age), it remains firmly located within the Christian culture of his time.

For over a century following Shakespeare's death, while his reputation as one of the greatest British writers grew exponentially, no one thought to comment on his religious beliefs, or lack of them. His Anglican Christianity was simply taken for granted. In the 1780s, scholars editing and interpreting Shakespeare's texts began to make observations on his use of religious language and his references to religious doctrines, but they did so without registering any sense of difficulty or awareness of doctrinal conflict. Whether it was Protestant Dr Johnson or Roman Catholic Alexander Pope, Shakespeare's early editors and critics saw nothing controversial about his religious opinions. When we consider that the intervening period, between 1616 and the 1780s, had seen religious divisions in Britain deepen to the point of civil war, the abolition of a Catholic-leaning monarchy and the execution of a king, the establishment of a Protestant republic, the restoration of the Stuarts, the deposition of James II for his Catholic sympathies, and the importation of a foreign Protestant monarchy – this assumption of an untroubled continuity of religious belief is perhaps remarkable. Eighteenth-century intellectuals seem to have found Shakespeare's religious beliefs both congenial and uncontroversial.

Around the middle of the nineteenth century, about the time Christianity began to come under attack from new scientific discoveries and theories such as evolution, scholars began to assert that Shakespeare's religious beliefs were of an orthodox Protestant complexion, and that he was a representative product of a Protestant "Golden Age" of culture and political stability governed by Queen Elizabeth I. Simultaneously, other scholars began to claim that Shakespeare grew up in a still largely Roman Catholic context that had not really been supplanted by the Reformation. At the same time the more enduring and influential hypothesis that Shakespeare was agnostic in matters of religion began to emerge. It was argued that he had the wisdom and prescience to understand that many of the doctrinal and liturgical controversies of his time were historically relative, and of no fundamental importance. In 1866 the *Edinburgh Review* characterized Shakespeare as a man who avoided the bitter struggles of the Reformation – the repeated "lurching between Rome and Geneva" – that he "became impatient with the harbour to which he was moored by the accidents of birth, and set sail for the wider ocean of humanity". Scottish historian Thomas Carlyle concurred in his "Goethe" essay: "Shakespeare is no sectarian". Here Shakespeare has been reinvented as a typical free-thinking, non-sectarian, and humanist Victorian intellectual.

The view of a Shakespeare who fitted comfortably within the Elizabethan Protestant religious settlement remained the dominant paradigm until after the Second World War, when it was replaced by more secular, sceptical, agnostic, and atheist critical interpretations. Thus today most contemporary Shakespeare criticism and scholarship, if directed towards religious matters at all, is likely to demote the sectarian question, "Was Shakespeare Protestant or Catholic?" to the more fundamental question of belief: "Was he religious at all?" Where Christians such as Samuel Johnson and Alexander Pope saw Shakespeare as a Christian like themselves, the modern Anglo-American Shakespeare scholar, more likely to be an atheist or agnostic, prefers to see him as a secular humanist, for whom religion was no more than a social construct. Many scholars today assume that religion did not play a very large role in Shakespeare's vision of life, and that he might have kept his personal religious opinions to himself simply because they were either uncontroversially orthodox, or almost indifferent, not only to sectarian controversies, but to the ultimate truths of religion.

It is sometimes assumed that because doctrinal conformity to the reformed church was, in Elizabethan England, compelled by law, and sometimes by force, that a quiet conformism was the only sensible way of living. Yet the religious behaviour of other dramatists very close to Shakespeare suggests that his orthodoxy was if anything unusual, and that his was much more of a choice between different available confessional positions. Christopher Marlowe, a huge influence on the early Shakespeare, seems to have recklessly and unashamedly identified himself as an atheist. Shakespeare's friend and rival, Ben Jonson, made a very public conversion to Catholicism, and an equally public recantation. Thomas Middleton, with whom Shakespeare collaborated on several plays, including *Macbeth*, clearly had leanings towards Calvinism. The more typical lot of the Elizabethan dramatist, then, is to have been as troubled, and troubling, about religion, as about other matters such as politics and morality. Shakespeare's orthodoxy seems, if anything, unusual for his time.

Again, it is often believed that because the state kept a tight control over the public drama by a system of prior approval and censorship that dramatists were well advised to avoid dealing with matters of religious doctrine on stage. And yet they didn't. Marlowe's relatively small output includes a metaphysical play about man, God, and the devil (*Doctor Faustus*); a play about Judaism and Christianity (*The Jew of Malta*); and a play about the St Bartholomew's Day Massacre, a landmark event of the Reformation (*The Massacre at Paris*). Ben Jonson mercilessly satirized the religious views of city Puritans in several of his plays. Shakespeare's adherence to the doctrine of the reformed Church of England again seems atypical rather than middle of the road; the outcome of deliberate choice, rather than a passive acquiescence in the status quo.

Shakespeare may have kept his religious opinions to himself because they were too controversial to be made public without courting the kind of trouble Marlowe seems to have invited. One possible inference of this kind is that he was in reality a Catholic – entirely possible when we consider the religious character of his background, his parents, his professional circle, together with the various allusions to his Catholicism. He might have lived, as many did, as a "church papist", outwardly conforming to the Church of England, avoiding the taking of Communion when he could (there is some circumstantial evidence that this may have been the case when he was living in Southwark, London, around 1600, though the evidence is necessarily negative), while hiding rather than disclosing his true religious feelings.

Scholars have been attracted to much more dramatic explanations. Some believe that Shakespeare might have been a fully fledged member of the Catholic underground that was clearly so busy all round him – attending secret masses and communicating with Catholic priests. He might have been drawn even deeper into that clandestine world, approaching close to the borders of conspiracy. This theory produces a dissident, nonconformist Shakespeare who seems in many ways more agreeable to modern readers than a quietist middle-of-the-road Anglican.

Or his notorious reticence about religion might have cloaked a more dangerous possibility, which is that of the atheism professed by his colleague Marlowe, and covertly by some advanced intellectuals of the time. He might have said nothing about his personal religious faith because he had none. There are certainly characters in his plays, as we shall see, who approximate to this position. Given the overwhelmingly Christian character of his work, this interpretation has been surprisingly common in Shakespeare criticism and scholarship. This may be because our secular and largely atheistic academic culture has sought to find its own reflection in the literature of the past. After all, if Shakespeare is a universal genius, and we belong to that section of the population (in the United Kingdom 25 per cent) who profess no religion, shouldn't he have no religion either? How could the work of a Christian author be presented as universally valid if all religions are equally meaningless? The possibility of an atheist Shakespeare at least deserves some consideration in the light of *King Lear*'s bleak and nihilistic vision of an apparently godless universe.

The recent revival of interest in the religious character of Shakespeare's works, the so-called "spiritual turn" in Shakespeare studies, has been dominated mainly by a revival of the "Catholic Shakespeare" theory, which has been given new impetus by major critics such as Stephen Greenblatt and Richard Wilson. A Catholic Shakespeare, who must have existed in an environment of intellectual dissent and covert resistance, has appealed to modern readers more strongly than the alternative of Shakespeare as a middle-of-the-road, conforming Anglican. More recently, critical and scholarly work has started to revisit the elements of Protestantism in Shakespeare's life and work, especially given that his religious culture, and the church to which he belonged, was overwhelmingly Protestant, Lutheran, and Calvinist.

My own view, to be argued and demonstrated in the pages that follow, is that Shakespeare was, both as a believing individual and as a writer, a faithful Protestant. But he was Protestant in the way that the Church of England was, and still is, Protestant. His Protestantism entailed a clear differentiation from many aspects of Roman Catholicism, without committing, as some Reformation thinkers did, to a wholesale rejection of its model of personal piety. He was Protestant in the way that *The Book of Common Prayer* is Protestant, combining as it does the language of Catholic tradition with the new reformed doctrines of Luther and Calvin. He looked back on the Catholic past with nostalgia rather than bitterness, with affection rather than rancour – as did the Elizabethan religious settlement, and as does the Church of England today – while at the same time committing to Protestant soteriology as the true path to salvation. From the polemical jest in *Love's Labours Lost* (1597) referring to the Protestant doctrine of salvation by faith alone – "my beauty will be saved by merit!/O heresy in fair, fit for these days!" (*Love's Labours Lost*, 4.1.22–3), to Shakespeare's Last Will and Testament, in which the dying man hopes to be saved "by the only merits of Jesus Christ my Saviour", Shakespeare's life and works reveal a manifest, and increasingly orthodox, Protestant form of Christianity.

CHAPTER ONE

"FAITH ALONE": THE REFORMATION

In order to understand the historical context of the religious environment in which Shakespeare lived, worked, thought, and believed, it is necessary to understand the English Reformation. The Reformation was a complex and wide-ranging series of revolutions within Christianity that took place across a few decades of the sixteenth century and which permanently affected church government, theology, access to the holy Scriptures, collective worship, and individual devotion, and had far-reaching implications for politics, ethics, and culture, including of course literature and drama. And though it is difficult to speak of the Reformation, especially in a brief introduction, without oversimplifying it, few people would dispute that something momentous happened between 1517, when Martin Luther mounted his first challenge to the church's authority, and 1563, when the Council of Trent consolidated the Catholic response familiarly known as the Counter-Reformation. Certainly the world into which Shakespeare was born in 1564 would not have been the same without these radical, decisive, and permanent changes.

The Reformation was essentially a European event. Its major thinkers and ideologues were Europeans – the German

Martin Luther, the Swiss Huldrych Zwingli, the Frenchman John Calvin. The Protestant challenge to the papal church's authority, and the subsequent separation of Protestant churches from Rome, happened first on the Continent. I will be concerned in this book mainly with the Reformation in England, where it touched directly upon Shakespeare's life and work. But it is also necessary to sketch its European origins, and to take account of some international developments, especially in France and in Italy, that impinged on Shakespeare himself, influenced the character of his own religious beliefs, and which are visible in his dramatic works.

Although there were earlier currents, and even movements, of reform within the Catholic Church, the Reformation proper can reasonably be dated from 1517, when Augustinian friar Martin Luther nailed his Ninety-five Theses ("Disputation on the Power and Efficacy of Indulgences") to the door of the castle church in Wittenberg. Luther was Professor of Theology ("Doctor of Bible") at the new university, later to be fictionally attended by Shakespeare's Hamlet and Horatio. His main target was the church's system of indulgences, which promised remission from punishment in purgatory in exchange for the performance of good works, or a financial payment. Neither doctrine has any precedent in Scripture, and many at the time considered the church's system to be little more than a money-making racket. So Luther was tapping into genuine reservations, shared by some Catholics, about the church's teaching on the crucial issues of penance and satisfaction.

If the church would not reform so manifest an abuse as the sale of indulgences, Luther began to realize, it must be fundamentally wrong about other things as well. His objections to the church's teaching that people could be saved by acquiring "merit" in the eyes of God, led him to the conclusion that faith alone was sufficient for salvation. "The just shall live by faith" (Romans 1:17), said St Paul. Luther preferred to add "by faith alone". The basis of faith lay in the Scriptures, not in any non-scriptural doctrines of the church, and we are saved not by our own merits, but solely by the grace of God, expressed through the redeeming sacrifice of Christ. Luther followed St Paul: "Not by the works of righteousness, which we had done, but according to his mercy he saved us, by the washing of the new birth, and the renewing of the holy Ghost" (Titus 3:5). Catholic tradition, derived from St Augustine, combined justification with sanctification: man could be transformed by his own good works into a creature acceptable to God. Luther recognized no such possibility. No Christian can ever guarantee his own salvation, however many good works he may do, however much merit he may accumulate. Humanity remains entirely sinful, and is rendered righteous only by God's saving intervention. Righteousness, Luther said, is "imputed" to sinful humanity, rather than earned or deserved. Luther's metaphor imagines Christ as a bridegroom taking a sinful, damned soul as his bride. Each takes possession of what the other brings to the marriage: Christ assumes humanity's sin, and in exchange bestows ("imputes") the free gift of grace.

Christ is full of grace, life, and salvation. The soul is full of sins, death, and damnation. Now let faith come between them and sins, death, and damnation will be Christ's, while grace, life, and salvation will be the soul's; for if Christ is a bridegroom, he must take upon himself the things which are his bride's and bestow upon her the things that are his. If he gives her his body and very self, how shall he not give her all that is his? And if he takes the body of the bride, how shall he not take all that is hers?

On Christian Liberty, 1520

Humanity remains *simul justus ac peccator* – a justified sinner. These radical ideas led to the formation of the central Protestant principle of the "solae": *sola fide, sola scriptura, solus Christus* (faith alone; Scripture alone; Christ alone). These are all that is necessary to salvation.

In 1521 the pope excommunicated Luther, whose response was to publicly burn the bull of excommunication in Wittenberg, and to publish a series of pamphlets releasing believers from obedience to canon law, reducing the seven sacraments to three (baptism, the Eucharist, and penance). Required to recant at the Diet of Worms, Luther refused: "Here I stand, I can do no other". Under the protection of the Elector Frederick of Saxony, Luther continued his campaign of reform and translated the New Testament into German. His was not the first German translation, but it became the most important. Vernacular translation of the Bible, already sponsored by Catholic reformers within the church – Erasmus was able to read the Bible in Dutch – became a key insistence of the Protestant Reformation. The Catholic Church retained the Latin "Vulgate" translation (right up to 1964, when the Second Vatican Council gave permission for parts of the Mass to be celebrated in the vernacular), and early vernacular Bible translators were persecuted. William Tyndale's English translation of the New Testament was the first to appear in print, and he was executed by Henry VIII for heresy. Only two years later, Henry licensed the English-language Great Bible, largely based on Tyndale's work, for use in churches, to be followed in 1568 by its successor the "Bishops' Bible". The English Bibles that supplied Shakespeare with hundreds of references and allusions had been current in the English church for only four decades before his birth. Yet up until the mid seventeenth century, more Bibles were printed and sold in England than anywhere else in Europe. Biblical quotations made their way into common speech, and the literature of the age is saturated with the English Bible.

Unlike the writings of earlier reformers, Luther's works were printed and published, using the new technology invented by Johannes Gutenberg that enabled radical ideas to be much more widely disseminated. The Reformation had begun. Eventually Luther's ideas were codified in 1530 in the "Augsburg Confession", which clearly set out the doctrinal principles of Lutheran Protestantism. The Confession affirms belief in the Trinity, original sin and its redemption through baptism, the reconciling efficacy of the incarnation, justification by faith, and the centrality of preaching. It accepts only two sacraments, baptism and the Eucharist, which it defines as containing the real presence of Christ in the bread and wine. The Augsburg Confession is a useful document, as it clearly differentiates Lutheranism not only from the Catholic Church, but also from other varieties of Protestantism that diverged much further from the traditional faith in the name of reform.

In Switzerland, Huldrych Zwingli agreed with Luther that Scripture was the only basis for truth, and that the pope had no real authority. He managed to obtain the support of the town council of Zurich to reform the church in the city: in 1524 images were removed from churches, clerical celibacy was abolished, and the following year a vernacular Communion service replaced the Latin Mass, administered not from an altar but from a wooden communion table, using wooden vessels. The people received the wine traditionally reserved for the clergy, as well as bread, in order to conform exactly to the institution of the Eucharist at the Last Supper as narrated in the Gospels. There were only two sacraments: baptism and Communion. Holy Orders and episcopacy were replaced by the ministry of pastors. Marriage became a civil ceremony.

In this case the switch from a universal obedience to Rome, to an independent Protestant church preaching and practising reformed doctrine, was both rapid and decisive. Simultaneously those who wanted reform to go further began to form recognizable groups, such as the Anabaptists who argued logically that infant baptism had no precedent in Scripture, and believers were baptized as adults (as is the case in the modern Baptist church). The spread of Reformation ideas in Germany precipitated the Peasants' War of 1524, led by the radical preacher Thomas Muntzer, whose thinking went beyond Luther's faith in Scripture to a belief in the "inner word" of private revelation. The revolt was brutally crushed, and Muntzer tortured and executed. In 1525 Luther had published a pamphlet encouraging the German princes to suppress the peasantry, an indication of how fast the tide of Reformation swelled, and how quickly Lutheran radicalism became conservative. Luther's teaching, particularly in its emphasis on direct personal reading of the Scriptures, in practice encouraged an independence of interpretation that far exceeded his own conception of reform.

The success of the Reformation did not lie in such popular "bottom-up" resistance, but in the emergence of political elites who saw advantage in adopting reformist (or, as Lutheranism came to be known, "evangelical") ideas. The princes of northern Germany welcomed the Protestantization of their churches, as did the Scandinavian kingdoms in the 1530s. It became possible within the Holy Roman Empire for self-governing states to decide for themselves on religious matters. The relations between church and state had fundamentally and irrevocably altered.

The Protestant states began to organize: in 1531 an alliance was formed by an agreement named after the town of Schmalkalden. Then in 1546, the year of Luther's death, the Holy Roman Emperor Charles V attacked the Schmalkaldic League, and secured a temporary victory. The Reformation began to be pushed back. The Protestant states rallied, and in 1555 the Peace of Augsburg concluded an agreement based on the principle *"cuius regio, eius religio"* ("your religion is that of your ruler"). This allowed Protestant and Catholic territories to exist side by side. Religious diversity was recognized, at least in Germany. At the same time it became necessary for anyone unprepared to accept their ruler's religion to move in order to find freedom of worship. And so began an age of emigration for religious reasons, and a population of religious refugees (one of whom, as we shall see later, became Shakespeare's landlord).

John Calvin's reform of the Swiss town of Geneva was radical enough to have been called by some scholars a "second Reformation". The urban authorities were attached to the Zwinglian model, in which city magistrates controlled the church. Calvin preferred a church independent of the state, governed by a "consistory" of ministers, magistrates, and lay "elders", who would control church discipline and regulate morality. Calvin's power-base included many Protestant refugees from other states fleeing persecution, such as John Knox, who was escaping the Catholic regime of Mary Tudor. Knox later (1559) led a revolt against Queen Mary Stuart, and established a Calvinist church in Scotland – the church in which Shakespeare's king and patron James I was raised. Calvin's influence spread quickly to neighbouring France, producing the Protestant religious minority known as Huguenots. In the Spanish Netherlands Calvinism became the doctrine of anti-imperialist resistance, one side in the religious wars that eventually divided the Netherlands between Protestant Holland and Catholic Belgium.

By the end of the sixteenth century the Church of England was very strongly inflected towards Calvinism. *The Book of Common Prayer* codified much Calvinist doctrine, and most of the clergy were of Calvinist persuasion. The basic principles of Calvin's theology had become the official doctrine of the English church. The knowledge of God was not inherent in humanity, and could be discovered only in Scripture: *sola scriptura*. The world was ruled by a providence through which God works His will, quite unaffected by independent human agency. Humanity since the fall of Adam had been infected with original sin, which can be redeemed only through the intervention of divine grace working through the sacrifice of Christ: *solus Christus*. Christ atones for sin, and justifies humanity by a grace that comes only from God, and is in no way dependent on human action. The knowledge of God in Christ is faith only: *sola fide*. In faith humanity finds the possibility of repentance, and thus remission from sin. We can then know spiritual regeneration, which takes us back towards the state of holiness enjoyed by humanity before the fall. Complete perfection, however, remains unattainable, so the human soul will always be the arena of a conflict between grace and sin. Finally there is Calvin's doctrine of predestination: some human beings are predestined to salvation, "elected" or chosen by God; others are born to damnation or abandonment. There is no choice in this, and no freedom of the will; it is God's decision, and human beings can do nothing to alter their soteriological status.

§

In 1560, just before Shakespeare's birth, England, Scotland, Denmark, Sweden, and Norway were all Protestant states. Germany was perhaps 80 per cent Protestant, and the Reformation had taken firm hold in France, the Netherlands, and Eastern Europe. By 1620, a few years after the time of Shakespeare's death, the Catholic Church and the Holy Roman Empire had revived, reasserted the traditional faith, and subjugated many Protestant powers. The landmark event in this process, known negatively as the Counter-Reformation, or more positively as Catholic Renewal, was the Council of Trent (1545–63). Initially the Council concentrated on codifying Catholic doctrine to distinguish it from Protestant "heresy", and went on to introduce institutional reforms. In terms of doctrine Trent uncompromisingly condemned Protestant ideas like justification by faith: "If anyone saith that by faith alone the impious is justified... let him be anathema." Trent rejected the Protestant insistence that only Scripture was necessary to salvation, and bestowed salvific efficacy on the traditions of the church, while affirming the Latin Vulgate Bible as the "authentic" form of Scripture. The Council standardized the Mass – the "Roman Rite" embodied in the *Roman Missal* published from 1570 to 1964 – and produced a common catechism for lay believers; tackled many abuses in church government; and introduced seminaries for the training of the clergy. Young Catholics from Protestant countries like England would flock to these seminaries in countries such as France. The Inquisition was set up as early as 1542, and an Index of prohibited books drawn up in 1559. The Catholic Church took on a spirit of renewal and evangelism: the Jesuit order had been established by Ignatius Loyola in 1534. Jesuit missionaries represented a powerful force in Europe, infiltrating Protestant nations such as Sweden and England, as well as preaching across Germany and Poland. Jesuit missionaries also play a significant, though ambiguous, role in the Shakespeare story.

The Council of Trent fixed the number of sacraments at seven: baptism, confirmation, marriage, ordination, extreme unction, penance, and the Eucharist. As we have seen, Protestants had already reduced these to two – the only ones with scriptural justification: baptism, based on Christ's own baptism in the River Jordan; and the Eucharist, instituted by Jesus himself at the Last Supper. The Catholic Church insisted on retaining all its traditional sacraments. In Catholicism baptism remained a literal cleansing of the child from original sin by the infusion of sanctifying grace. Calvinists saw baptism more as a declaration of faith by the community, and a ritual of reception for the new member. These changes can be traced in successive editions of the English *Book of Common Prayer*. Lutherans continued to regard baptism as necessary for salvation. The Anabaptists argued logically that since only adults, not children, are baptized in the Scriptures, Christian practice should follow that example. This of course rendered baptism a voluntary option, rather than an imposed requirement, allowing the adult believer to choose. What was regarded as an extremist heresy in the sixteenth century is now the normal model for all mainstream Christian churches in Western Europe.

Luther initially retained penance, the confession of sins to a priest in exchange for absolution, but later abandoned it as inessential (this compromise left its mark on *The Book of Common Prayer*). Catholicism maintained the practice of securing penance by confession before taking the Eucharist. In 1614 the now-familiar closed confessional box was ordered to be used in all dioceses. It had already been introduced by the archbishop of Milan, Cardinal Borromeo, a leading figure of the Counter-Reformation, and a name that will crop up later in Shakespeare's family life: confession became private, anonymous, inscrutable. In Protestant churches this practice was replaced by a communal general confession.

Possibly the most significant conflict between Catholic and Protestant views of the sacraments lay in observance of the Eucharist. The Catholic understanding of this sacrament remained unaltered. At the Last Supper Christ had commanded his apostles to eat bread, and to drink wine, in remembrance of his coming sacrifice. "This is my body," he had said; "this is my blood". The Catholic Mass is not a memorial ritual, or a symbolic performance, but a re-enactment of Christ's own sacrifice upon the cross. By repeating the words of institution – "this is my body"; "this is my blood" – the priest causes bread and wine to become the body and blood of Christ, a process theologically known as "transubstantiation", the conversion of one thing into another by the application of divine power. In the Aristotelean terms used in the sixteenth century, the bread and wine superficially remained the same in terms of their "accidents" – their outward semblance; but changed absolutely within, in their constitutive "substance". Once consecrated, the bread becomes the "host" (from the Latin *ostia*, sacrificial victim) that bears the presence of Christ: an object of adoration. The elevation of the host is literally a revelation of God to the people. Through the Mass the grace of God is transmitted directly to its worshippers, and a Mass could be regarded as a "work" of grace, applied to particular objectives such as the relief of a soul in purgatory.

The Protestant challenge to the Catholic Mass is probably the most acute and extreme controversy of the Reformation, and the main reason why we still have separate Catholic and Protestant churches. For Protestants, Christ's sacrifice on the cross was a once-for-all event that could never be revived or re-enacted by priestly agency. It was nothing less than blasphemy to believe otherwise. Transubstantiation was a relic of mediaeval scholasticism that seduced the people into worshipping an idol, one of the graven images forbidden by Scripture. The most radical overhaul of the Eucharist was undertaken by Zwingli, who declared that the words of institution – "this is my body" – could not be taken literally, since the bread on the table at the Last Supper was manifestly not Christ's body, any more than is the consecrated wafer on the altar. Hence the Eucharist must be understood metaphorically, with "is" meaning "represents", as a symbol of the covenant between God and his people. The Mass became commemorative rather than sacrificial, a reminder of a sacrifice that could take place only once and for ever, and so Zwingli insisted on the use of the ordinary bread that must have been used at the Last Supper, rather than special wafers, and the wine that had previously been reserved for the priesthood was offered to all communicants.

Luther, on the other hand, retained a fundamental belief in the real presence. In a public debate between Luther and Zwingli organized by Philip of Hess in 1529, Luther is said to have written in chalk on the table before him the text "*hoc est corpus meum*" ("this is my body"), as if the words themselves were intransigent obstacles to any radical redefinition. The Lutheran understanding of the Eucharist came to be called "consubstantiation", a process in which there is a real presence, but one that exists in parallel with the consecrated elements, rather than being inherent within them. Calvin promoted a higher view of the Eucharist than Zwingli's symbolic conception, retaining the notion of real presence, while denying that divine grace infiltrated the bread and wine. Christ enters into the souls of true believers at the Eucharist, and in this way divine grace is "received".

Despite these more-or-less radical redefinitions of the Mass, observance of the Eucharist remained at the heart of Protestant worship and theology. No longer a sacrifice conducted on an altar, the Lord's Supper became "Holy Communion", a collective act of reception, celebrated around a wooden table. The community would come together in the Eucharist, responding to the divine "invitation", confessing their sins in common, and putting aside their differences and disagreements. All communicants should be at ease with their own consciences, and in charity with their neighbours, since Christ's instructions at the Last Supper also included the *mandatum*: "A new commandment give I unto you, that ye love one another: as I have loved you, that ye also love one another" (John 13:34). Notwithstanding these doctrinal controversies, in Protestantism the Lord's Supper remains a great and solemn celebration, a sacramental means of purifying grace, and a model of godly community.

§

As indicated above, the Protestant Reformation was primarily a European event. But its impact was experienced in England both rapidly and decisively. In the 1530s Henry VIII separated the Church of England from Rome, denying the authority of the pope, and splitting England from the Roman Catholic faith. This was effected via a series of Acts of Parliament passed between 1532 and 1534, including the Act of Supremacy. The church became a national church, no longer part of Roman Catholic Christendom, and immediately more open to the theological and liturgical influences of Protestant reformers such as Luther, Zwingli, and Calvin.

Today the story of the Reformation, though not offered as such, has become familiar through popular TV dramatizations such as *The Tudors* (2007–2010) and the historical novels of Hilary Mantel, *Wolf Hall* (2009), and *Bring Up the Bodies* (2012). The initial catalyst for Henry's decisive break with the past was of course his wish to have his marriage to Catherine of Aragon annulled, so he could marry Anne Boleyn and produce a male heir. Anne herself had Protestant sympathies, and patronized reformers in the church. Prior to this crisis, Henry had been a pious Catholic, and a staunch defender of the Roman Church: in 1521 he published a book, *The Defence of the Seven Sacraments*, rebutting Luther as a heretic. In recognition of this Pope Leo X awarded him the title "Defender of the Faith". Thus the title retained by all subsequent English (Protestant) monarchs initially referred to a defence of the pre-Reformation Roman Catholic Church! But after the fall of Lord Chancellor Cardinal Wolsey (1529), men of reformist sympathies like Thomas Cromwell and Thomas Cranmer came to prominence. They assisted Henry in resisting challenges to his programme from within the church. It was Cromwell who drafted the Act in Restraint of Appeals (1533), which declared that

> *this realm of England is an Empire, and so hath been accepted in the world, governed by one Supreme Head and King having the dignity and royal estate of the Imperial Crown of the same, unto whom a body politic, compact of all sorts and degrees of people divided in terms and by names of Spirituality and Temporality, be bounden and owe to bear next to God a natural and humble obedience... .*

England was an independent nation, with a national church, of which the king was the supreme head. In 1534 the Act of Supremacy made Henry "Supreme Head on earth of the Church of England", contrary to any "usage, custom, foreign laws, foreign authority and prescription". Cranmer was appointed archbishop of Canterbury, and promptly declared Henry's marriage to Catherine to have been against the law of God. Henry married Anne Boleyn in 1533, and later that year Princess Elizabeth was born. Both Henry and Cranmer were immediately excommunicated by the pope.

As historians have shown, the Reformation in England did not come out of the blue, and the Roman Catholic Church was not exactly what the Protestant reformers claimed it was. There were early movements of theological radicalism from within the church, such as Lollardy in the fourteenth century. This was based on the leadership of Oxford professor John Wycliffe, who attacked the privileged position of the clergy and the use of excessive ceremony in the church, and translated at least parts of an English Bible that was circulated (in manuscript, since this was prior to the invention of printing) under his name. His followers stressed the relative importance of Scripture over the traditions of the church, and the preaching of the word over the sacrament of the altar. Sir John Oldcastle, the proto-Protestant martyr whose name is confusingly entangled with Shakespeare's Falstaff, led a rebellion in 1415 that was brutally crushed by Henry V. At the same time there were movements for reform inside the Roman Church, led by men such as Desiderius Erasmus and Thomas More, who criticized the corruption of the clergy and the abuses of ecclesiastical power.

Despite these historical possibilities, the Reformation in England succeeded only as a "top-down" process engineered by the government and facilitated by the existence of the English common law, which easily replaced the legal writ of Rome. Henry VIII supervised a process of reform from 1536, beginning with the abolition of feast days and the suppression of votive images and pilgrimages. In the same year began the dissolution of the monasteries, which transferred land and wealth from the church to the crown and the aristocracy. These changes were resisted by popular uprising and by armed force, including the rebellion known as the Pilgrimage of Grace (1536), but invariably Henry got his way. Even before this process was completed, however, the king had changed tack, and began to act against the dissemination of Protestant ideas, banning discussion of the sacrament and clerical marriage. The year 1539 saw the passing in Parliament of the Six Articles, reaffirming Roman Catholic practices such as transubstantiation, clerical celibacy, and the importance of confession to a priest. The execution of Cromwell (1540) was a landmark event in this temporary movement against the forces of reform.

The death of Henry VIII in 1547 paved the way for the most far-reaching phase of England's Reformation, led by the young King Edward VI's advisers, under his uncle, the powerful Lord Protector Edward Seymour, Duke of Somerset. As we shall see, this high water mark of the Reformation starts to impinge on Shakespeare's life in noticeable ways. In 1547 Parliament passed and enforced an iconoclastic "injunction against images", requiring the destruction of all images, shrines, stained glass, and statues in churches. Crosses were taken down, rood lofts (a partition between chancel and nave bearing a representation of the crucifixion) removed. Restrictions were placed on the use of vestments, and chalices were melted down. The clergy was no longer required to be celibate. Processions on feast days, palms on Palm Sunday, ashes on Ash Wednesday were all forbidden. The endowments providing Masses for the dead, known as chantries, were abolished.

In 1549 Cranmer introduced the first *Book of Common Prayer* in English, which obligated English parish churches to conduct their worship entirely in the vernacular tongue. Although to some extent a translation of the Catholic Latin Mass, the doctrinal position of *The Book of Common Prayer* was unashamedly Protestant. It introduced into the Mass a reformist conception of the gifts, no longer offered to God as a sacrifice, but rather serving as a "remembrance of his most fruitful and glorious Passion". Holy Communion was celebrated from 1550 on wooden communion tables, rather than stone altars. In 1552 the second English prayer book replaced the first, making the Protestant theology of the Eucharist abundantly clear:

Almighty God our heavenly father, which of thy tender mercy didst give thine only son Jesus Christ, to suffer death upon the cross for our redemption, who made there (by his one oblation of himself once offered) a full, perfect and sufficient sacrifice, oblation, and satisfaction, for the sins of the whole world, and did institute, and in his holy Gospel command us to continue, a perpetual memory of that his precious death, until his coming again…

The Mass was thus replaced by Holy Communion, a commemorative rite acknowledging the once-for-all efficacy of Christ's sacrifice of himself on the cross. Through the official Books of Homilies (*Certain Sermons to be Read in Churches*), Cranmer preached the Lutheran and Calvinist scheme of salvation in addresses on Scripture, original sin, justification, salvation, and good works. "Righteousness… embraced by faith" was "taken, accepted and allowed of God for our perfect and full justification". Good works were not to be undertaken "to be made good by doing of them". During this period the Church of England was genuinely transformed. *The Book of Common Prayer* determined the pattern of church liturgy and its transmission in vernacular English. The Edwardian reformation was codified into forty-two articles, later revised as the "Thirty-nine Articles" (1571) that became included in subsequent editions of the prayer book. These Protestant articles of belief remain the doctrinal cornerstone of the Church of England. They begin with creedal statements about the Trinity, the incarnation, the resurrection, the Holy Spirit, then proceed to an uncompromising insistence on the primacy of Scripture:

> *Holy Scriptures containeth all things necessary to salvation: so that whatsoever is not read therein, nor may be proved thereby, is not to be required of any man, that it should be believed as an Article of the Faith, or be thought requisite or necessary to salvation.*

(Article VI)

The Articles define original sin, free will, and justification by faith:

> *We are accounted righteous before God, only for the merit of our Lord and Saviour Jesus Christ, by faith, and not of our own works or deservings…*

(Article XI)

The Catholic emphasis on "good works" is rejected for a causal explanation of virtue: good works naturally flow from faith, but curry no favour with God:

Albeit that Good Works, which are the fruits of Faith, and follow after Justification, cannot put away our sins, and endure the severity of God's judgment, yet are they pleasing and acceptable to God in Christ, and do spring out necessarily of a true and lively Faith; insomuch that by them a lively Faith may be as evidently known, as a tree discerned by the fruit.

(Article XII)

Faith is the tree, and good works the fruit. The fruit is a natural outgrowth, but the tree can stand without dependence on its own fruit.

The Articles then countermand alternative forms of Christian belief, including both Roman Catholic and more radically Protestant opinions. They reject "Purgatory, Pardons, Worshipping and Adoration", together with the "invocation of the Saints" as "Romish" superstitions (Article XXII). But they also target for condemnation lay preaching, speaking in tongues, and the holding of goods in common – all principles of the Anabaptist sect. Contrary to Catholic doctrine, the sacraments are defined as two in number:

Sacraments ordained of Christ be not only badges or tokens of Christian men's profession, but rather they be certain sure witnesses, and effectual signs of grace, and God's good will towards us, by the which he doth work invisibly in us, and doth not only quicken, but also strengthen and confirm our Faith in him.

There are two Sacraments ordained of Christ our Lord in the Gospel; that is to say, Baptism, and the Supper of the Lord.

Those five commonly called Sacraments, that is to say, Confirmation, Penance, Orders, Matrimony, and Extreme Unction, are not to be counted for Sacraments of the Gospel...

(Article XXV)

This first phase of the English Reformation came to a shuddering halt when, in 1553, Edward died, and was replaced by his half-sister Mary Tudor, daughter of Catherine of Aragon and a devout Roman Catholic. Mary I restored the English allegiance to Rome, and repealed Reformation legislation. Cranmer was tried for heresy, and burned at the stake. The Protestant culture built up over the two preceding reigns was naturally defended, especially by its clergy, and Mary had to resort to persecution to extirpate Protestant resistance. A total of 283 Protestants were burned at the stake for heresy; some 7 per cent of all those executed for heresy throughout Europe in the sixteenth century. These atrocities were immortalized in John Foxe's *Acts and Monuments of the Church* (1563 and regularly revised and reprinted), better known as the *Book of Martyrs*, where they served subsequent generations as graphic and moving examples of Catholic persecution. Mary attempted to reverse the progress of the Reformation, and to restore the traditional faith in terms of devotional practice and popular piety as well as church government and liturgy. Historians are divided on the impact of her Counter-Reformation; some argue that she liberated Catholic forms of belief that had only been suppressed by the Tudor reformation, and might, if she had lived longer, have permanently restored the "old faith"; others that such patterns of belief had soon been eroded, that there was no widespread popular support for Catholic practices, and that England's future lay with a reformed church and state. Certainly Mary's counter-reformation ceased with her death, childless and without a Catholic successor, in 1558.

Elizabeth I assumed the throne determined to avoid the extremes of her siblings' religious alterations. As the Catholic Church regarded her as illegitimate, and therefore unqualified to rule, she could hardly in any case have been a Roman Catholic. But she had no intention of revisiting the turbulent unrest associated with the Edwardian reforms. Together with her senior advisers, such as William Cecil, she set about creating an inclusive church of England, that allowed for diversity of opinion, and excluded only Catholics loyal to the pope (who did not recognize her legitimacy), and Protestant "separatists" who pursued reform until it took them out of the church altogether. Naturally this diversified church embraced religious tensions, which were eventually to surface in the English Civil War. But during Elizabeth's forty-five-year reign (1558–1603) the Church of England was held together, as it was in the reign of her successor James I (1603–25). Thus Shakespeare (1564–1616), unlike his parents, remained throughout his life a member of a unified and inclusive, though diverse, Church of England.

The Elizabethan church was established first through a Reformation Bill. Its purpose was "to restore the Supremacy of the Church of England to the Crown of the Realm", and to impose "a uniform order of religion". The intention was to reintroduce the 1552 *Book of Common Prayer*, and to define the Communion as a memorial rather than a sacrifice. However, the strength of Roman Catholics in the House of Lords prevented the bill from passing into law. Following protracted debates, the Acts of Supremacy and Uniformity finally made Elizabeth Supreme Governor of the Church of England, and forced people to attend Sunday service in an Anglican church with a new version of *The Book of Common Prayer* (1559). The latter removed abuse of the pope from the litany, and allowed for both consubstantial and transubstantial beliefs in the presence of Christ in the Eucharist.

Roman Catholicism persisted, under conditions of considerable difficulty, and partly of necessity, underground. There were Roman Catholic priests and laity still practising their religion in defiance of the Elizabethan settlement, refusing

to take the oath of uniformity. Only one significant act of internal resistance marked a serious effort to restore the old faith, the Rising of the Northern Earls in 1569, which failed in its attempt to depose Elizabeth and replace her with Mary Stuart. A more serious threat came from the danger of external invasion by Spain with the intention of deposing Elizabeth and restoring Catholicism – but the Spanish Armada which threatened England in 1588 was dispersed by wind and tide, and Elizabeth survived. In 1570 she was excommunicated by Pope Pius V, and tensions deepened. Fines for refusal to attend church were raised. It was now treason to be loyal to Rome. Catholic priests were outlawed, and many executed. Despite such reprisals, Catholic resistance remained sufficiently strong to support, in 1605, the conspiracy of the Gunpowder Plot, aimed at assassinating Elizabeth's Protestant successor James I.

Contemporaries liked to see Elizabeth as a heroine of the Reformation, as (to apply Shakespeare's description of Henry V) "the mirror of all Christian kings". Theologically she was Lutheran rather than Calvinist, believing in a physical rather than spiritual presence in the Eucharist. She tended to swear by old Catholic oaths, was fond of images, and preferred a celibate clergy. She refused to place as much weight on preaching as some of her more Protestant bishops. For as long as possible she spared the life of Mary Queen of Scots, and refused to allow anti-Catholic ideology to determine foreign policy. The approach she preferred was one of tolerance, cautiousness, and realpolitik. Such programmes of political compromise tend to satisfy moderates, and incense extremists. Both Catholic and Puritan dissatisfaction with the Church of England increased during her reign, challenged the authority of her successor, and erupted into civil war in the reign of Charles I.

§

The following chapters will trace the impact of the Reformation on Shakespeare's works, via detailed discussion of individual plays, preceded by a chapter on religion in Shakespeare's own family and personal life.

CHAPTER TWO

"THE ONLY MERITS":
THE FAITH OF WILLIAM
SHAKESPEARE

This, then, was the religious condition of the England into which William Shakespeare was born on (or around) 23 April 1564. But what do we know of his own religious beliefs, his creedal commitment, his personal confession? What was the faith of William Shakespeare?

Our first problem is that of understanding the religious world in which Shakespeare lived. Today some 60 per cent of British people identify themselves as Christians, while 25 per cent say they have no religion at all. A much smaller minority of 8 per cent profess other faiths such as Judaism, Hinduism, Sikhism, and Islam (statistics from 2011 UK census). Despite the obvious inference from these figures – that religion remains the majority position, and Christianity the majority religion – our laws require equal treatment for all religions, and none, and tend to be applied in favour of minorities: the law often gives non-religious or anti-religious views, such as humanism and atheism, an advantage – in public affairs – over Christianity, disproportionate to the numbers who profess them as a matter of personal conviction. Diversity of belief is assumed, encouraged, and even compelled by law, custom, and social convention.

In Shakespeare's England, there was only one religion – Christianity – and only one permitted doctrinal form of that religion, that was embodied in the reformed Church of England. Church attendance was obligatory, and, as mentioned earlier, absence from church was punishable by fine, or even imprisonment for repeated offences. Since Henry VIII's Act of Supremacy (and excepting the reign of Catholic Mary Tudor, 1553–58), the monarch was the supreme head of the church: hence loyalty to one entailed conformity with the other. At times of political crisis (such as the period following the 1570 papal bull *Regnans in Excelsis*, which declared Elizabeth I a heretic for blocking "exercise of the true religion", accused her of "usurping monster-like the place of the chief sovereign of the church of England", and released her subjects from loyalty to her), these two obligations became indistinguishable, and the practice of an alternative confession such as Catholicism could become synonymous with treason.

So if we ask what did people believe in sixteenth-century England?, there is one categorical answer: they believed in the creeds of the Church of England, and their religious behaviour was wholly prescribed by its liturgical practice, specifically through *The Book of Common Prayer*. But since this orthodoxy was forcibly compelled, we might suspect that the personal beliefs of many people actually diverged from that orthodoxy. We certainly know this to be partly true, since many who conformed to the church ("church papists") continued to believe as Catholics, and there were many who tried whenever they could to stay away from the church and its sacraments ("recusants"). At the same time, many Protestants found the Church of England still essentially unreformed, and attempted in various ways to dissent from it, while formally remaining members to escape persecution. *The*

Book of Common Prayer began as a vehicle of the Reformation, but was outlawed by Parliament in 1645, when Oliver Cromwell was Lord Protector, as being irredeemably Catholic.

It was of course understood that different faiths existed, and that foreigners would profess different beliefs. Islamic ambassadors from Morocco spent some six months in Elizabeth's court in 1600. A Jewish scholar, Jacob Barnet, could be employed in Hebrew studies at the University of Oxford. But as in other parts of Europe, and as in the case of Shakespeare's Shylock, Jews were expected to convert to Christianity. The very public refusal of Jacob Barnet to complete his promised conversion resulted in his imprisonment. But compelled or required conversion is unlikely to efface original religious beliefs.

In such an environment religious diversity is not dispelled, but merely driven underground. People continue to believe in very different ways, but are for the most part unable to reveal their true beliefs. The Elizabethan church attempted to offer the kind of via media that would enable varieties of religious opinion to occupy a common ground, and routinely avoided prying into matters of personal belief: Elizabeth herself said she had no intention of "making windows into men's souls". But religious controversy simmered under the surface and broke out at various times into sectarian violence or open defiance of both the church and the state.

Our second problem is that of the Shakespeare biography. Unlike many other writers of the time (not all), we have almost no direct historical evidence as to what he thought or felt about anything. Religious opinions of many kinds are expressed in his plays, but they are all put in the mouths of the characters who speak them, and cannot safely be attributed to the author. Even the famous sonnets, which have often been read autobiographically, are more often interpreted now as a kind of impersonal lyrical drama, and provide no certain evidence about the poet's inner life. His friend Ben Jonson wrote many lyric poems containing elements of religious doctrine and spiritual emotion, which enable us to reconstruct something of his personal piety. Shakespeare never did. While Shakespeare the author is ubiquitously visible via his works, Shakespeare the private man remains largely mysterious and unfathomable.

People often say that very little is known of Shakespeare's life. Scholars retort that in fact a great deal is known about him for a literary figure from that period, though there are yawning gaps such as the so-called "lost years" of 1585–92, during which no documentary evidence survived. The problem is not lack of information, or even its lack of comprehensiveness, but its the kind of information we do have, which is all public, and not private. There remains not a single letter, or diary entry, or reported conversation that might provide us with such insight; nothing except for a court record from 1612, discussed below, documenting Shakespeare's oral deposition in a case at the Court of Requests, which in itself is tantalizingly opaque and self-effacing; and Shakespeare's Last Will and Testament, which of course he signed, and which contains what some consider to be a significant statement of religious belief.

In what follows I will sketch the religious character of Shakespeare's family and social background, and gather the historical evidence that throws light on Shakespeare's religious beliefs. Was he a believing Christian? If not, an agnostic or atheist? If so, a Catholic or a Protestant?

§

The lives of Shakespeare's parents were strongly marked, in various ways, by the Reformation. His father, John, was born a Roman Catholic (as were all English people before 1534), during the reign of Henry VIII (1509–47). John Shakespeare was born in 1530, a few years before Henry's Act of Supremacy

(1534) put an end to the dominance of the Roman Church in England. His wife, Mary Arden, was born some few years later, probably around 1535. They both lived through the brief and zealous reign of Protestant Edward (1547–53), during which the reformers were in the ascendant, and the equally fundamentalist regime of Mary Tudor (1553–58), who restored the practices of the old faith. By the time of Shakespeare's birth in 1564, Elizabeth had restored Protestantism to the Church of England. Attendance at Protestant services, based on *The Book of Common Prayer*, was obligatory, and absence punishable by fine.

We know far less about Shakespeare's mother Mary than we know of his father, which is not unusual for this period. It is probable that she came from a strongly Catholic family. When her father died in 1556 he bequeathed his property to his daughter, and his soul to "Almighty God and to our blessed lady saint Mary and to all the holy company of heaven". The vicar who attested the will would soon be removed from his office for adherence to the old faith. Mary Arden, named after that same Blessed Virgin, may have been related to a family that remained fiercely loyal to Catholicism – that of Edward Arden of Park Hall near Stratford-upon-Avon, who was executed by hanging, drawing, and quartering in 1583 for plotting against the queen, Elizabeth.

Shakespeare's father, John, was a successful businessman who, alongside his primary trade of glove-making, dealt in wool and other agricultural produce, invested in both land and property, and operated as a money-lender. He held a number of civic offices in Stratford, culminating in the position of high bailiff (a kind of mayor), to which he was elected in 1568. All those who held civic office had to be church members in good standing, and had to swear an oath of allegiance to Queen Elizabeth as supreme head of the church. Shakespeare's father must have done so, from the year of Elizabeth's accession 1559, in order to become successively affeeror (an officer responsible for assessing fines), burgess, and chamberlain in Stratford.

John certainly had to prove his loyalty to the Tudor Protestant state in practical ways. In 1559 an iconoclastic royal injunction from the government of the newly crowned Elizabeth demanded the removal of all signs of "superstition" and "idolatry" from places of worship. A series of paintings on the walls of Stratford's Guild Chapel, including a magnificent "Doom" or depiction of the Last Judgment, were defaced, covered over with whitewash; the old rood loft taken down; and a Communion table erected to satisfy Protestant liturgical requirements. The job was supervised by John Shakespeare, who was chamberlain of Stratford 1563–64. It is listed in his accounts: "Item paid for defacing images in the chapel, two shillings".

In the discharge of his public offices, John Shakespeare behaved, therefore, in every respect as a loyally Protestant servant of the reformed Tudor church and state. But he was born a Roman Catholic, and his first public offices, such as that of borough ale-taster (1558), were obtained during the reign of Catholic Mary Tudor. What then was his private religion? In 1592 he was twice named in government reports as a "recusant", one of those who "refuse obstinately to resort to church". He pleaded, as others also did, that his absences were to avoid being arrested for debt. He was always in debt, but never apparently arrested: he was certainly appearing at public functions around the same time. He may therefore have been, as the evidence directly suggests, a recusant Roman Catholic.

There is one historical document that provides substantive evidence that John was privately a Catholic, though its validity is strongly disputed. It is claimed that in 1757 a bricklayer working on what had been John Shakespeare's house (now "Shakespeare's Birthplace") found hidden between the rafters and the roof an extraordinary document. It was a six-page, hand-written testament of Catholic faith, in fourteen articles, each page signed in the name of John Shakespeare. The original document is now lost, and its contents were preserved in an eighteenth-century copy that is at least partly a forgery. In fact the document was suspected as entirely fraudulent, until later discoveries corroborated its authenticity. It was composed by the cardinal archbishop of Milan, Carlo Borromeo, and used as a propaganda tool in the spiritual campaigns of the Counter-Reformation, within which he was a prominent figure. Thousands of copies had obviously been distributed to Catholics by travelling Jesuits, with the intention of reinforcing and encouraging them to make public profession of their faith.

The document signed by John Shakespeare was most likely brought to England by the Jesuit missionaries Edmund Campion and Robert Persons, who travelled from Rome via Milan, where they met with Cardinal Borromeo. Campion stayed with Sir William Catesby only twelve miles from Stratford; the house of the Catholic magnate, father of Robert Catesby the Gunpowder Plotter, must have served as headquarters for the Jesuit's evangelical mission. The pamphlets would have been distributed to Catholic believers, including John Shakespeare, at secret Masses, or meetings, or even clandestine home visits. Signing such a document clearly makes Shakespeare's father not only a recusant, but a devout and dedicated, Roman Catholic.

"John Shakespeare's Spiritual Testament" was an illegal and comprehensively heretical declaration of faith in Catholic doctrine, in the sacraments, and in purgatory, together with prayers to the Blessed Virgin and the saints:

> *I, John Shakspeare, do protest that I will also pass out of this life, armed with the last sacrament of extreme unction: the which if through any let or hindrance I should not then be able to have, I do now also for that time demand and crave the same; beseeching*

his divine majesty that He will be pleased to anoint my senses both internal and external; with the sacred oil of His infinite mercy, and to pardon me all my sins committed by seeing, speaking, feeling, smelling, hearing, touching, or by any other way whatsoever.

As indicated above, the genuineness of John Shakespeare's spiritual testament has been disputed, but the explanations that challenge its validity are elaborate and unconvincing. According to this document Shakespeare's father remained, despite his respectably Protestant public life, privately a devout Roman Catholic.

There is little doubt that a strong network of kinship, acquaintance and proximity linked the Shakespeares with the Catholic community in Warwickshire, a county where government commissioners found most of the common people still to be stubbornly papist. Along with the Ardens, local families like the Treshams, the Winters, and the Catesbys kept the old faith alive. Arden was executed for sheltering John Somerville, convicted of conspiracy against the queen's life: John Shakespeare's testament was probably hidden at that time from government officers who were searching local houses for incriminating evidence against Catholics. The other family names mentioned are also those of the conspirators – Thomas Tresham, Thomas and Robert Winter, Robert Catesby – who, after the failed Gunpowder Plot, retreated to the Midlands, and either died or were captured fighting for their lost cause. There is strong circumstantial evidence to suggest that Shakespeare's father and mother both remained to some degree Catholic, possibly "church papists" who outwardly conformed, concealing their true faith, occasionally attracting the attention of the authorities at times of religious crisis, but managing in the end to conceal their true beliefs behind a façade of consistent public conformity.

For in terms of the public commitment to Protestantism

required of every one of Elizabeth's subjects by the Acts of Supremacy and Uniformity (1558–59), the Shakespeare family conformed. John Shakespeare baptized his last seven (of eight) children, and buried two of them, in the rites of the reformed church. He managed the iconoclastic vandalism of the Guild Chapel in 1559, and some years later, as deputy bailiff of Stratford, agreed to the sale of the chapel's property, including copes, manuaries, and vestments. We have no idea how he felt about these examples of loyalty and conformity. They might have been at odds with his personal confession of faith. Or he may have discharged them without scruple, having renounced the old faith in favour of a Protestantism that could be lived by more easily.

§

Since the mid nineteenth century, some scholars and critics have been arguing that Shakespeare inherited his father's Catholicism, and concealed it behind a façade of Protestant orthodoxy. The idea that William was a closet Catholic appears very early in the historical record. In some manuscript notes, jotted down in the later seventeenth century, Richard Davies, chaplain of Corpus Christi College, Oxford, wrote of William Shakespeare:

> *Aetat 53. He died Apr. 23 1616 probably at Stratford, for there he is buried, and hath a Monument on which lays a Heavy curse upon anyone who shall remove his bones. He died a papist.*

What did it mean, to "die a papist"? Perhaps Davies meant that Shakespeare was born a papist, and never left off being one to his dying day. Once a Catholic, always a Catholic, as the old saying goes. Davies was a successful career Anglican, and may have viewed Shakespeare critically as a stubborn recusant, who lived and died incorrigibly in the old faith. He may have been saying something like: "A great man of letters he may have been, but he lived and died a papist."

It is not known for certain whether Shakespeare attended Stratford Grammar School, though the plays and poems could not have been written without a good school education, or the equivalent in expensive private tuition. Nicholas Rowe's 1709 biography states that Shakespeare's father had to withdraw him from school to help in the shop, but that at least implies that for some time he was there. Of the six masters presiding at the Stratford Grammar School during the period in which Shakespeare may have attended, four were Roman Catholics. Two came from Oxford colleges with strong Catholic connections: St John's (Jesuit martyr Campion's college) and Brasenose. Simon Hunt, who may have been one of William's teachers, retired in 1575 to the seminary at Douai, France, and became a Jesuit. John Cottam was brother to Thomas Cottam, a Jesuit associate of Campion who was tortured in the Tower of London, and executed in 1582.

Shakespeare's twin children Hamnet and Judith were clearly named after their godparents, Stratford neighbours Hamnet and Judith Sadler, who were definitely Catholics (named, as they were, Catholic recusants). If Shakespeare did "retire" to Stratford in his later years (he certainly spent more time there, though still active in London, and of course died there) then he can only have found this papistical atmosphere congenial. His daughter Susanna was cited in May 1606 as a recusant who failed to appear at Easter Communion (though it should also be pointed out that she married a Protestant, Dr John Hall).

Shakespeare's literary career also kept him in close association with Catholics. His patron, and possibly close friend, the earl of Southampton, came from a prominent Catholic family. Southampton's father assisted Campion, and Catholics were sheltered in his mother's house in Holborn. Southampton's tutor and confessor was Jesuit poet and martyr Robert Southwell. There may have been a link between Shakespeare and Southwell, who was put to death in 1595. Southwell may have been alluding to Shakespeare in a tract as "my loving cousin W.S.", and Shakespeare certainly used an image from his poem "The Burning Babe" in *Macbeth*. Early modern historian John Speed, in some remarks on the character assassinations of the Lollard knight Sir John Oldcastle (original of Falstaff) seems to have linked Shakespeare with Jesuit Robert Persons, referring to "the papist and his poet".

In 1613 Shakespeare purchased the Blackfriars Gatehouse in London. This property, formerly part of the dissolved Blackfriars Monastery, had remained in Catholic hands since the time of the Reformation and was notorious for Jesuit conspiracies, priest holes to hide fugitives, and covert Catholic activity. In his will Shakespeare bequeathed the Gatehouse to his daughter Susanna, and ensured that John Robinson, who lived in the house, could continue his tenancy. In the same year Robinson's brother entered the seminary at the English College in Rome.

Despite the weight of this evidence, it all remains circumstantial, and neither proves nor disproves William Shakespeare's Catholicism. There is no doubt that Shakespeare was closely hemmed in by Catholicism, but that does not in itself make him a Catholic. At the very centre of this whirlwind of conspiracy, recusancy, resistance, and rebellion, Shakespeare keeps his silence.

Most of the effort engaged in proving Shakespeare's Catholic connections has, perhaps significantly, focused on the "lost years", during which period he virtually disappears from the biographer's view. Between the record of his marriage, 1582, and the first mention of him in the London theatre, 1592, nothing is known of where he was, or what he was doing. He fathered children, the twins who were baptized in 1584, and he may have been personally involved in a Stratford family property case brought to court in 1587.

Proponents of the "Catholic Shakespeare" theory believe they may have found this lost Shakespeare in the shape of a William Shakeshaft who served Catholic gentleman Alexander Hoghton at his seat of Hoghton Hall in Lancashire. This idea was first suggested as far back as 1937, and has recently gained a new lease of life. In his will, Alexander Hoghton recommended for employment as players Shakeshaft and Fulk Gillom to Sir Thomas Hesketh, a patron of the drama. Many scholars believe that this Shakeshaft was the seventeen-year-old Shakespeare, and indeed that this is how he found his way into the theatrical profession. Stratford schoolmaster John Cottam was from Hoghton, and could have recommended young Shakespeare to the Hoghtons as a private tutor (John Aubrey stated that Shakespeare had been "a scholemaster in the country"). Campion and his Jesuit mission certainly travelled to Lancashire, so it is possible that Shakespeare was recruited by them into some kind of Catholic service. The theory depends however on a combination of circumstantial evidence and the identification of Shakespeare with Shakeshaft. It all remains at the level of speculation rather than fact.

§

Although William inherited through his parents a divided, and divisive, religious culture, he lived all his life in complete conformity with the Church of England. He was baptized in Holy Trinity Church, Stratford, on 26 April 1564, according to the rites of the 1559 *Book of Common Prayer*, restored to the church after Mary's Catholic interregnum by the newly crowned Elizabeth. Shakespeare had all his children similarly baptized, and his son Hamnet buried, by the rites of the reformed church. Unlike his father, and his daughter Susanna, William Shakespeare himself was never cited for recusancy. In 1608, the Stratford parish register shows he stood godfather to a child of Henry Walker. In 1614 he entertained a preacher at his Stratford house, New Place, and the local council paid his expenses. As lessee of the Stratford tithes, one of his property investments, he became a lay rector of Holy Trinity Church. On his death in 1616 he was buried in the chancel of the church, where a monument to his memory was erected some time between 1616 and 1650. His wife, Anne, was buried with him when she died in 1623.

Between 1602 and 1604 Shakespeare lodged in the house of a Protestant family, refugee Huguenots from France, in Cripplegate. His landlord, Christopher Mountjoy, was a member of the French Protestant church. This association brought Shakespeare into court on 11 May 1612, as a witness to an alleged breach of promise between his landlord and the landlord's apprentice, Stephen Bellott. Bellott was claiming a dowry of £50 he claimed was promised by Mountjoy when the apprentice married the landlord's daughter. The court record is the only instance of Shakespeare's own words having been written down.

11 May 1612

William Shakespeare of Stratford upon Avon in the County of Warwick, gentleman, of the age of xlviii years or thereabouts sworn and examined the day and year aboue said...

As the court record indicates, Shakespeare was sworn in as a witness, and therefore gave evidence on oath. Although other witnesses described Shakespeare as extensively involved in the courtship and marriage of his landlord's daughter, he deposed that he could recall no details of the financial arrangements. This record shows a clerk of the court writing down Shakespeare's actual words.

To the fourth interrogatory this deponent saith that the defendant promised to give the said complainant a portion in marriage with Mary, his daughter, but what certain portion he remembereth not, nor when to be paid, nor knoweth that the defendant promised the plaintiff two hundred pounds with his daughter, Mary, at the time of his decease, but saith that the plaintiff was dwelling with the defendant in his house, and they had amongst themselves many conferences about their marriage which [afterwards] was consummated and solemnized and more he can [not depose.]

Given the extraordinary capacity of Shakespeare's literary memory, his training as an actor, and the evidence of his financial acumen, this amnesia seems hard to believe. If he was lying on oath, this would indicate that he had no religious scruples about forswearing, contrary to the church's Articles of Religion: "a man may swear when the Magistrate requireth, in a cause of faith and charity" (Article XXXIX). But this is pure speculation. Perhaps his memory really was failing: four years later he would be dead.

In 1607, William's brother Edmund, an actor, died and was buried "in the church" (not the churchyard) of St Saviour in Southwark. The burial register shows that the funeral was accompanied also by an "afore noon knell of the great bell". The interment and passing bell cost "20 shillings". It is probable that William paid this fee for his deceased younger brother.

William knew the Bible in different translations, but after 1596 quoted more frequently from the Protestant Geneva Bible (even sometimes quoting from its marginalia, indicating a reading knowledge rather than an auditory acquaintance). The Geneva Bible was both common and popular, so not hard to come by, but the timing of Shakespeare's more regular recourse to the Protestant translation may suggest that he used a copy that was present in the Mountjoy household.

The most strikingly Protestant detail to be found within the historical records of Shakespeare's life is in his Last Will and Testament.

In the name of God, Amen. I, William Shakespeare… in perfect health and memory, God be praised, do make and ordain this my last will and testament in manner and form following. That is to say, first, I commend my soul into the hands of God my Creator, hoping and assuredly believing, through the only merits of Jesus Christ my Saviour, to be made partaker of life everlasting, and my body to the earth whereof it is made.

"Through the only merits of Jesus Christ my Saviour" is clearly a Protestant formulation. *Solus Christus*, Christ alone, as we saw in the previous chapter, was one of the fundamental principles of the Reformation: that salvation was possible only through the undeserved grace and mercy of God, manifested through the redemptive sacrifice of Christ, and not from any merit or righteousness displayed by humanity. As St Paul writes in his epistle to Titus:

Not by works of righteousness, which we had done, but according to his mercy he saved us, by the washing of the new birth, and the renewing of the holy Ghost
Which he shed on us abundantly through Jesus Christ our Saviour…

Titus 3:5–6

This doctrine is clearly stated in the Thirty-nine Articles:

We are accounted righteous before God, only for the merit of our Lord and Saviour Jesus Christ… we are justified by faith only…

(Article XI)

Scholars have argued that the expression "through the only merits of Jesus Christ my Saviour" was formulaic in different forms (it even appears in a specimen will that is included in a contemporary book of legal forms), and may not have held any personal doctrinal significance to Shakespeare. But the weighty meaning of the document itself, written a few days before Shakespeare's death; its proportionate value in the relatively small collection of biographical records illustrating his life; and its consistency with a career of apparently blameless orthodoxy, all surely suggest that he died affirming a Protestant faith in the unique efficacy for salvation of Christ's sacrifice.

§

That Shakespeare was a Christian writer, at least by virtue of cultural context and literary inheritance, is indisputable. The Christian Bible was one of his primary sources. He cited in his plays some forty-two books of the Bible: eighteen from the Old Testament, eighteen from the New, and six from the Apocrypha. Whole books have been written on Shakespeare's indebtedness to the Bible, and estimates of the number of allusions he used range from about 1,200 to somewhere around double that number (since not all the possible allusions can be regarded as definite). He certainly quoted and alluded to the Bible more than any other Elizabethan dramatist. Among his favourite biblical books were Genesis, Matthew, and Job, while the most-frequently cited is the Psalms. The biblical story in which he seems to have found the most dramatic potency is that of Cain and Abel from Genesis, which he mentioned more than twenty-five times.

Shakespeare must therefore have regularly consulted the Bible as he was writing, and recalled it from memory. Regular church attendance would have familiarized him with the annual lectionary of Scripture that prescribed the reading of the (almost) complete Old Testament once, and the New (apart from Revelation) twice. The complete Psalms, Shakespeare's preferred biblical source, were read through once every month. The "Great Bible" was issued in 1539, and used in churches until the 1570s, when it was officially replaced by the Bishops' Bible, published in 1568 and revised in 1572. The psalms remained unchanged across the revised translations. The Bishops' Bible is the version Shakespeare would have heard in church, and memorized (if that is how he acquired this material), and it is certainly one of the translations from which he quotes. He also used the Protestant Geneva translation, which was published in 1560, and became very popular, though it was never formally used in churches. So when we find Shakespeare quoting from the Geneva version, that tells us that he read the Bible, as well as heard it. When Henry V reprimands Falstaff with the exhortation "know the grave doth gape/For thee thrice wider than for other men" (5.5.53–54), he echoes the Bishops' Bible translation of Isaiah 5:14: "Therefore gapeth hell, and open her mouth marvellous wide". But when in the same play Mistress Quickly garbles Romans 15:1, "bear with one another's confirmities", she inadvertently puns on the Geneva version ("infirmities"), as the Bishops' Bible reads "frailties".

Always of course the theological and liturgical basis of Christianity, in Reformation England the vernacular Bible became universally familiar through its centrality in Protestant doctrine (*sola scriptura*) and church liturgy, and as a printed and published text it became a cornerstone of common literacy. Its influence, therefore, fell upon every English subject, whatever their private religious beliefs or personal confession. So the fact that Shakespeare knew the Bible well, and used it as a narrative and dramatic source, does not in itself tell us about his personal belief system. It does on the other hand suggest that he was a church-attending and Bible-reading Christian.

And while the Christian Bible was the text that distinguished Christian belief from other faiths, it was also the arena in which Christians of different persuasions fought one another over matters of doctrine and belief. The earliest English translations of the Scripture were associated with the proto-Protestant Lollard movement, and the first printed version was published (starting in 1526) by William Tyndale, a reformer influenced by Luther as well as Erasmus. The Bishops' Bible consists mainly of Tyndale's translation. The Geneva version appeared with marginal commentaries, some written by Calvin, that interpreted the Scriptures in the light of Calvinist doctrine. In 1582 a "Catholic" New Testament was published at Rheims. It is tempting to identify contrasting confessional positions in these different publications.

Shakespeare certainly used the Bishops' Bible and the Geneva version, and he may have shown awareness of the Rheims New Testament. But any attempt to find in these allusions evidence of a confessional preference is quickly frustrated. His usage seems to be eclectic, "catholic" with a lower-case initial, rather than dogmatic. We cannot, for example, definitively say he used the Geneva version in later stages of his career when and after lodging with the Mountjoys, as he also used it before the period in question (1602–1603).

All we can say in general terms is that Shakespeare's plays are pervaded by the presence of the Bible. In the chapters that follow I will frequently discuss examples of his biblical quotations and allusions to show how they work in their context. These discussions will demonstrate that biblical reference in Shakespeare is evidence of more than a general familiarity and a shared biblical literacy. They also show his imagination to have operated in fundamentally religious ways, and furthermore, they show his religious beliefs converging on a particular confessional position: a Lutheran and Calvinist Protestantism.

The other foundational religious text that hovers continually behind Shakespeare's works is *The Book of Common Prayer*, specifically the 1559 version introduced after Elizabeth's accession. Arguably more important than the Bible in terms of its influence on everyday religious practice, the prayer book prescribed not only the offices for morning and evening prayer, and the celebration of Holy Communion, but also the rituals for the conduct of christenings, marriages, and funerals – holy baptism, the solemnization of matrimony, and the burial of the dead. It is possible to think of Shakespeare reading the Bible in the same way as a modern sceptic would, perceiving it as a work of literature rather than the revealed word of God, mining it for useful material rather than believing in its religious message. The prayer book is different, since it is not a literary text for reading, but a liturgical script for performance, like the text of one of Shakespeare's own plays. One can read the Bible in much the same way as one can read any other book. But frequentation of *The Book of Common Prayer* entails participation in communal rites, active involvement in the performance of liturgy, and willing assent to the demands and obligations of a religious practice. We don't know how often Shakespeare attended church, especially in London; though in view of his involvement in the management and business of Holy Trinity Stratford, it would have been strange for him not to be a regular churchgoer. And while we cannot know with any certainty exactly how Shakespeare acquired his biblical knowledge, we can state categorically that his formal religious practice was shaped and governed by *The Book of Common Prayer*. He was married, his children were baptized, his son, his brother, and his father were buried, all by the rites prescribed in the 1559 *Book of Common Prayer*. That Shakespeare was within the environment of the prayer book on at least an occasional, and more likely a regular, basis is one of the few certainties to be relied on in this field of inquiry.

In *As You Like It* Orlando and Rosaline participate in a mock marriage, with Celia playing the part of a priest.

> *Rosalind.* Come, sister, you shall be the priest and marry us. – Give me your hand, Orlando. – What do you say, sister?
> *Orlando.* [*to Celia*] Pray thee, marry us.
> *Celia.* I cannot say the words.
> *Rosalind.* You must begin, "Will you, Orlando" –
> *Celia.* Go to. Will you, Orlando, have to wife this Rosalind?
> *Orlando.* I will.
> *Rosalind.* Ay, but when?
> *Orlando.* Why now, as fast as she can marry us.
> *Celia.* Then you must say "I take thee, Rosalind, for wife."
> *Orlando.* I take thee, Rosalind, for wife.
> *Rosalind.* I might ask you for your commission; but I do take thee, Orlando, for my husband. There's a girl goes before the priest; and certainly a woman's thought runs before her actions.

(4.1.106–19)

The mock ceremony imitates exactly the language of the marriage service in *The Book of Common Prayer*. "Will you, Orlando, have to wife this Rosalind?" copies the prayer book's "Wilt thou have this woman to thy wedded wife?" In both texts the answer is "I will". Celia prompts Orlando with the prayer book's words, "I take thee, N., to my wedded wife"."I take thee, Rosalind, for wife." This is just a small example demonstrating Shakespeare's exact verbal knowledge of the prayer book. In the pages that follow, similar usages will be adduced as evidence of Shakespeare's religious commitment and practical piety. In fact it would not be wide of the mark to claim that the faith of William Shakespeare was the faith of the English Bible and *The Book of Common Prayer.*

§

In the pages that follow, I will examine a selection of Shakespeare's plays to discover their religious content, and to unearth anything that might tell us more about his faith. The plays are not of course confessional statements, and tend to treat religious doctrines with some circumspection. On the other hand I think it possible to construct from close examination of these works a non-systematic religious persuasion on the part of their author.

Critical studies of religion in Shakespeare tend to range widely across his work, selecting for attention passages that refer explicitly to the church, the clergy, religious doctrine, or language. But Shakespeare's plays are creative unities that need to be seen or read as a whole. If there is a religious vision in Shakespeare, it will be found not in isolated references and allusions scattered throughout his work, but in the overall structural design, and in the painstakingly assembled dramatic and poetic detail of the individual play. This book takes the play as the basic unit of religious thought and feeling, which is the normal method for teaching and researching Shakespeare's works. The selection of plays offered here is not of course complete or exhaustive, and other plays would reveal slightly different inflections of religious affirmation. But the general argument, evidenced from the representative selection of plays discussed below – histories, comedies, tragedies – should prove sound and convincing. Shakespeare may have grown up in the shadow of recusant Catholicism, but he committed to the Church of England and, far from reverting to any childhood Catholicism at the end of his life, grew more Protestant as he grew older.

CHAPTER THREE

"PATTERN TO ALL PRINCES":
THE FAMOUS HISTORY OF THE LIFE OF KING HENRY VIII

The story of the English Reformation is, for good or ill, identical to the story of the Tudor monarchy. The leading figures in any account of the English Reformation, whether historical or fictional, are not the great theological innovators such as Luther, Zwingli, and Calvin, who dominated the European Reformation, but a king, two of his wives and his three children. The British Reformation story is dominated by Henry VIII, Catherine of Aragon, Anne Boleyn; the leading churchmen who served them – Cardinal Wolsey, Thomas More, Archbishop Cranmer – and the three children of Henry VIII, by separate wives, who each in turn occupied the throne of England – Edward VI, Mary I, and Elizabeth I. Any consideration of the English Reformation must always entail a consideration of Henry VIII's dynastic and national ambitions, his marriage and divorce, and the religious convictions of his children and their advisers. These prominent Reformation figures happen to be the characters in one of Shakespeare's less familiar plays, and this specific crucible of historical change – King Henry's divorce from Catherine of

Aragon, his marriage to Anne Boleyn, and the birth of the princess Elizabeth – is its main theme. That play is *The Famous History of the Life of King Henry VIII*, written in Shakespeare's later years, possibly in collaboration with John Fletcher, and will serve as my starting point.

§

The primary source for *Henry VIII*, as for all of Shakespeare's historical plays, is Raphael Holinshed's *Chronicles of England, Scotland and Ireland* (1577, revised 1587), though the play also draws on other sources, such as Edward Halle's *The Union of the Two Noble and Illustrious Families of Lancaster and York* (1548), and John Foxe's *Acts and Monuments* (1597, revised 1583) – the polemical Protestant work more commonly known as the *Book of Martyrs*. These works of Tudor historiography are, in doctrinal terms, typical of the Protestant intellectual culture that flourished during Elizabeth's reign. All the main outlines of the Tudor Reformation narrative, common knowledge to anyone familiar with our many contemporary fictional and dramatic presentations of the Tudors, are present in Holinshed: the vanity and ambition of Cardinal Wolsey; his "vain pomp and show of dignity"; the king's troubled conscience over the legality of his marriage to Catherine; the queen's self-presentation as an object of pity – a "poor woman, and a stranger"; Henry's falling for Anne Boleyn; and Wolsey's plotting to steer the divorce in the direction he preferred, which was for the king to marry a French princess. Holinshed's narrative of the discovery of Wolsey's "treachery", his fall from power, and his tragic resignation is the one followed by Shakespeare and all subsequent historical and fictional narrators. We see the emergence, from the aftermath of Wolsey's fall, of Thomas Cromwell, and the ascension to royal favour of Thomas Cranmer. The play makes little direct use of Holinshed's extensive documentation of the religious changes outlined in the preceding chapter – of the Reformation itself – but it does arrive at the same conclusion. *Henry VIII* ends with the birth of the princess Elizabeth, an event celebrated by Holinshed (writing during Elizabeth's reign) as a divinely ordained blessing on the English people and the English nation:

> *From that time forward (God himself undertaking the*
> *tuition of this young princess, having predestinated her to the*
> *accomplishment of his divine purpose) she prospered under the*
> *lord's hand as a chosen plant of his watering, and after the*
> *revolution of certain years with great felicity and joy of all*
> *English hearts attained to the crown of this realm, and now*
> *reigneth over the same.*

"Predestinated" invokes of course John Calvin's providentialism. The play begins with Wolsey's power at its height, exemplified by the festivities surrounding the meeting in 1520 of Henry VIII and King Francis I of France, the conference known as the Field of the Cloth of Gold. Two noblemen discuss the proceedings in accents of ambiguous admiration. On the one hand it represented the summit of human pageantry, "the view of earthly glory". On the other hand it is described in various terms derived from the arts: a "painting", a "masque", a "fabulous story", too good to believe. This suggestion of synthetic display, of theatrical show, prepares the way for the revelation that the festivities were organized by Cardinal Wolsey, more to promote his own ambition than to display the power of the king. They are condemned as "fierce vanities" facilitated by a parvenu whose lack of ancestry and achievement compels him to narcissistically promote himself and his own career:

Spider-like,
Out of his self-drawing web, a gives us note
The force of his own merit makes his way –
A gift that heaven gives for him which buys
A place next to the king.

(1.1.62–66)

In the play's very first scene, then, Wolsey is criticized in the
authentic language of Reformation polemic and doctrinal
controversy. Wolsey is conscious of his own "merit" rather
than the saving grace of Christ. He does not accept grace from
heaven as a free gift, but uses it to "buy" power, influence, and
royal favour. The case against the cardinal is that he is primarily
concerned to make his own career, feather his own nest, spinning
his own advantage, like the spider's "self-drawing web". But the
play accentuates this condemnation with doctrinal overtones
drawn from the language of Reformation Protestantism. The
cardinal is just too Catholic: he believes in his own "merits", not
those of his saviour; he thinks grace is something bestowed on
him in return for those merits; and he believes he can buy his way
to righteousness. This negative assessment of Wolsey's motives
leads the noblemen to doubt the validity of the treaty agreed
between the kings, "a proper title of a peace, and purchased/At a
superfluous rate" (1.1.197–98). Wolsey's political machinations,
based as they are in his vanity and ambition, are bad for the
king, and bad for England.

Later in the same scene the duke of Buckingham – about
to become a victim of Wolsey's plotting – insistently links his
political double-dealing with his status as a senior Catholic
clergyman: "This holy fox… this cunning cardinal… our court-
cardinal":

> Let the King know… that thus the Cardinal
> Does buy and sell his honour as he pleases…

(1.1.190–93)

The repeated linking here of papal status and mendacity, Wolsey's pursuit of personal wealth rather than the good of church and state, and a running critique of the belief that honour, merit, and grace can be "purchased", lies firmly within the language of the English Reformation. Indeed the play features two of Shakespeare's only six uses of the word "reformation" (1.3.19 and 5.2.54), usually applied to denote an individual moral conversion rather than a general social movement, but also with a suggestion of the word's broader connotations. The later use of "reformation" actually occurs in a speech of anti-Protestant polemic from Bishop Gardiner, in turn copied from Foxe's *Acts and Monuments*, where Gardiner asserts that the kingdom is "infected with heresies", and that it was "dangerous to his highness to permit it unreformed". In the earlier reference the crown demands a "reformation" in the behaviour of courtiers who have absorbed French habits and manners: the realm is moving against European Catholic culture, and towards a Protestant nationalism.

The demise of Buckingham, engineered by Wolsey, foreshadows Wolsey's own fall. The cardinal is purging members of the nobility who challenge his authority, with scant respect for justice. On his way to execution Buckingham speaks a compelling language of forgiveness and reconciliation, drawn from familiar scriptural and liturgical sources:

> You few that loved me
> … Go with me like good angels to my end,
> And, as the long divorce of steel falls on me,

Make of your prayers one sweet sacrifice,
And lift my soul to heaven.

(2.1.73–79)

The strikingly felicitous phrase "the long divorce of steel" is of course Shakespeare's own invention, but the rest of the speech is drawn from religious sources. Buckingham echoes the Bible: "And ye shall make a burnt offering for a sweet savor unto the Lord" (Numbers 29:2); the psalter: "Let my prayer be directed in thy sight *as* incense, *and* the lifting up of mine hands *as* an evening sacrifice" (Psalm 141:2), and *The Book of Common Prayer*: "his one oblation of himself once offered... a full, perfect and sufficient sacrifice". He protests his innocence, but forgives his persecutors, as did Christ on the cross: "I heartily forgive 'em", wishing only that they had been "more Christians". The cardinal should be wary however of capitalizing on his downfall, lest his innocent blood should cry against him: "For then my guiltless blood must cry against 'em" (2.1.69).

Here Buckingham quotes directly from one of Shakespeare's favourite biblical moments – the murder of Abel by Cain in Genesis: "the voice of thy brother's blood crieth unto me, from the earth" (Genesis 4:10). Shakespeare refers back to this foundational biblical text throughout his career, finding in it a crucial nexus of associations between betrayal, violence, and haunting. Here Wolsey is cast in the role of Cain, his act of vindictive treachery sowing the seed of an evil harvest, and raising the ghost of a righteous tribulation. Although the play scarcely provides sufficient character development for Buckingham to be perceived as a man unjustly served by Wolsey's malice, his religious language here assumes the authority of Scripture as a basis for rebuking the cardinal's less than Christian behaviour, and his tragic fate foreshadows a parallel fall for the engineer of his misfortunes. In the words of an anonymous "Gentleman",

> O, this is full of pity, sir, it calls,
> I fear, too many curses on their heads
> That were the authors.

(2.1.137–39)

§

Following these preliminary scenes, the play then moves to its main business, and addresses the topic of the king's marriage to Catherine of Aragon. The same "Gentleman" prepares the audience by asserting that Wolsey himself is the prime mover of the divorce, his malice towards the queen founded on a resentment against the emperor (Catherine's nephew, Charles V) "for not bestowing on him, at his asking/The archbishopric of Toledo". We hear that Henry's conscience has been smitten by doubts about the legality of his marriage, since Catherine was married previously to his own late brother Arthur, and he has already met and been captivated by Anne Boleyn. Both the moral and opportunistic motives for the divorce, debated by the lord chamberlain and the duke of Norfolk, are left to lie side by side in the reader's mind:

> *Cham.* It seems the marriage with his brother's wife
> Has crept too near his conscience.
> *Nor.* No his conscience
> Has crept too near another lady.

(2.2.15–17)

Norfolk blames Wolsey for plotting against the queen, though later Henry himself makes it clear that in his view Wolsey has hindered rather than advanced the "king's great matter". During these central acts, Henry appears however to be completely under Wolsey's sway, calling him "the quiet of my wounded conscience", "a cure fit for a king". With the arrival from Rome of Cardinal Campeius, Henry's reliance on the apparatus of the Catholic Church is ever more strongly emphasized. The king's cause is supported, Wolsey affirms, by "Rome, the nurse of judgement", and Henry thanks "the holy conclave for their loves". At the same time we are given glimpses of Wolsey's subterfuge, when, for example, he welcomes Bishop Gardiner to the trial as "the king's" man, to which Gardiner replies, "But to be commanded/For ever by your grace" (2.2.118–19); whereupon the two men, according to the stage direction, furtively "*walk and whisper*".

In one of the play's liveliest scenes, Anne Boleyn is presented as a sympathetic observer of Catherine's sorrow, which has dissuaded her, Anne, from harbouring any ambitions of her own. A comical "Old Lady" companion vigorously satirizes Anne's modesty, insisting that given the opportunity of advancement, her conscience would expand like "soft cheverel" leather to accommodate her enlarged career prospects. News of the king's favour towards Anne is immediately brought to her by the lord chamberlain, who tells her she has, by the king's "grace", been created Marchioness of Pembroke, and is singled out for particular honour: "heav'nly blessings/Follow such creatures" (2.3.57–58). Anne responds with a becoming modesty:

> *Anne.* I do not know
> What kind of my obedience I should tender.
> More than my all is nothing: nor my prayers
> Are not words duly hallowed, nor my wishes
> More worth than empty vanities; yet prayers and wishes
> Are all I can return. Beseech your lordship,
> Vouchsafe to speak my thanks and my obedience,

As from a blushing handmaid to his highness,
Whose health and royalty I pray for.

(2.3.65–73)

Anne responds to this mark of the king's favour with a humble obedience that echoes the Virgin Mary's at the annunciation. The chamberlain then praises Anne in an aside to the audience:

[*Aside*] I have perused her well.
Beauty and honour in her are so mingled
That they have caught the King, and who knows yet
But from this lady may proceed a gem
To lighten all this isle.

(2.3.75–79)

The echoes of Scripture and liturgy sound very clearly in these lines. The chamberlain speaks like the Angel Gabriel announcing the incarnation to Mary: "heav'nly blessings/Follow such creatures", echoing Luke's "blessed art thou among women"; the counterpointing of images: "a blushing handmaid"; "a gem/To lighten all this isle" – further recalls the juxtapositioning of the Magnificat and the Nunc Dimittis in the evensong service from *The Book of Common Prayer*: "he hath regarded/The lowliness of his handmaiden"; "a light to lighten the Gentiles/And to be the glory of thy people Israel". Anne's is a distinctively Protestant kind of virtue: she claims no merit for herself; possesses nothing but prayers to return for the gift of "grace". From her, the lord chamberlain prophesies, will be born a child capable of bringing the light of truth to the nation, "to lighten all this isle". These specific liturgical echoes bestow an elevated religious quality on the dramatic moment, enabling it to transcend the rough comedy of the Old Lady's mockery. The king and the future queen are incorporated as actors into an unfolding religious history greater than themselves, as England ("this isle") begins to assume its providential destiny as a Protestant nation under the guidance of God.

§

By the end of Act 2 we know that Henry has lost his trust in Wolsey and in the ecclesiastical authority he represents, and has begun to repose his faith in Cranmer. In a revealing aside that closes the second act, the king identifies the untrustworthy Wolsey with Rome, and with cardinals in general:

> *King. [Aside]* I may perceive
> These cardinals trifle with me. I abhor
> This dilatory sloth and tricks of Rome.
> My learn'd and well-beloved servant, Cranmer,
> Prithee return. With thy approach I know
> My comfort comes along.

(3.1.232–37)

In Act 3 a conversation between the chamberlain, Norfolk, and Suffolk informs the audience that the king has discovered the full extent of Wolsey's treachery.

> *Norf.* In the divorce his contrary proceedings
> Are all unfolded, wherein he appears
> As I would wish mine enemy....
> *Suff.* The Cardinal's letters to the Pope miscarried,
> And came to th'eye o'th' King, wherein was read
> How that the Cardinal did entreat his holiness
> To stay the judgment o'th' divorce, for if
> It did take place, "I do," quoth he, "perceive

> My king is tangled in affection to
> A creature of the Queen's, Lady Anne Boleyn".

(3.2.26–8, 30–36)

Wolsey's contemptuous dismissal of Anne is then countermanded by another speech in her praise from Suffolk, who again portrays her as the gateway to a new national greatness – "from her/Will fall some blessing to this land, which shall/In it be memoriz'd" (3.2.49–51) – and again echoes the Magnificat: "For behold from henceforth/All generations shall call me blessed". Unaware of these developments, Wolsey is seen still plotting against the king, still hoping to arrange a marriage with the duchess of Alencon: "I'll no Anne Bullens [Boleyn] for him". The primary source of this opposition to the king's will lies in Rome: "speedily I wish to hear/From Rome". And in a most explicit and revealing speech, Wolsey aligns political with religious differences, revealing his allegiance to Catholic Rome, and locating both Anne and Cranmer on the opposite side of the Reformation divide:

> What though I know her virtuous
> And well deserving? Yet I know her for
> A spleeny Lutheran, and not wholesome to
> Our cause, that she should lie i'th' bosom of
> Our hard-ruled King. Again, there is sprung up
> An heretic, an arch one, Cranmer, one
> Hath crawled into the favour of the King…

(3.2.97–103)

"Spleeny" usually suggests a rash, passionate nature, and the naming of Anne as a Lutheran is taken straight from John Foxe: "the cardinal of York [Wolsey] perceived the king to cast favour on the Lady Anne, who he knew to be a Lutheran". The historical

Henry, we should recall, had been a militant anti-Lutheran. But in the play, and by this point, Protestantism has become associated with both the royal and the national interest, and with England's hopes for the future. When Wolsey so openly attacks both Anne and Cranmer as "heretics", the audience is surely expected to take a confessional side, and to recognize that the heretics of yesterday (like Elizabeth) can become the bearers of today's orthodoxy.

The play then moves to the king's public condemnation and humiliation of Wolsey. He has learned of the cardinal's immense accumulated wealth, so excessive it "out-speaks/Possession of a subject". Just as the monastic orders had been accused of focusing on earthly wealth rather than heavenly things, so Wolsey is condemned for the same reason: "his thinkings are below the moon", not "fix'd on spiritual object". First Henry requires Wolsey to "confess" (3.2.164) his loyalty, which the cardinal does, using the same terms as Anne when she responds to the king's generosity. Henry's grace, like God's, has been so liberally showered upon him that he can return only "allegiant thanks". A good Protestant answer. But then the king shows Wolsey an inventory of his, Wolsey's, personal fortune, and all the cardinal's schemes are laid bare. Aside to the audience Wolsey admits that his mendacity has been the instrument of his ambition, referring to "all that world of wealth I have drawn together/For mine own ends (indeed to gain the popedom/And fee my friends in Rome)". Included with the inventory is an intercepted letter written by Wolsey to the pope asking him to block the divorce. Wolsey's ascendance has reached its zenith, and he faces the inevitable fall:

> Nay then, farewell.
> I have touched the highest point of all my greatness,
> And, from that full meridian of my glory
> I haste now to my setting. I shall fall

Like a bright exhalation in the evening,
And no man see me more.

(3.2.223–28)

Wolsey is arrested and stripped of his office, and thrown to the mercy of the nobles who hate him. The litany of complaints to which they subject him is full of anti-Catholic language, in which Wolsey's treachery and financial impropriety are identified with his cardinal's robes and with Rome: "scarlet sin... a piece of scarlet... extortion... you writ to the Pope against the king... your holy hat". Wolsey has extorted wealth in order to "furnish Rome", "to the mere undoing of the kingdom". Wolsey's last great speech – "a long farewell to all my greatness" – concludes by his comparing himself to Lucifer, falling from the greatest height into the lowest depths: "he falls like Lucifer/Never to hope again" (3.2.371–72). Wolsey dismisses Cromwell so that his protégé will not be sucked into the maelstrom of his own fall, and counsels him to "fling away ambition":

Let all the ends thou aim'st at be thy country's,
Thy God's, and truth's. Then if thou fall'st, O Cromwell,
Thou fall'st a blessed martyr.
Serve the King...

(4.1.448–50)

Country, God, truth, in that order. Wolsey at last accepts that the nation houses both faith and the revelation that manifests it in the Church of England. And the *sine qua non* of these principles is: "serve the king", defender of the faith, absolute head of church and state. A set of Protestant loyalties has replaced the Catholic creed: "Country, God, truth, king" substitute for "Rome, God, truth, pope".

With Wolsey removed, the path is clear to Anne's coronation, reported in Act 4 by a group of "gentlemen". The ceremony shows Anne as a "saint-like" figure, so universally popular as to create around her an intense social unanimity: the spectators cram so closely together that no one can tell them apart: "all were woven/So strangely in one piece." Cranmer and Cromwell are now the king's trustworthy retainers. The nation is bound to the king via this new marriage, and via the establishment of the Protestant faith it has facilitated.

§

Opposition to Henry's programme remains strong, and the play's fourth act demonstrates the continuing resistance of men such as Bishop Gardiner, who sets out to continue Wolsey's mission to root out the Protestant "Lutheran" sect surrounding Anne. He tells Sir Thomas Lovell that the realm must be rid of the new queen and her reforming associates:

> it will ne'er be well …
> Till Cranmer, Cromwell – her two hands – and she,
> Sleep in their graves.

(5.1.30–32)

Cranmer, Gardiner asserts, is "a most arch-heretic", the heresy he promotes "a pestilence/That does infect the land", and has captivated the king. But the bishop has deliberately "incens'd the lords o' the council" against Cranmer, who is to be brought to trial, and interrogated over his "heretical" (that is, Lutheran) opinions. The king is well aware of this plot, and privately assures Cranmer of his royal favour: "Thy truth and thy integrity is rooted/In us thy friend". From behind the scenes he observes Gardiner and others mistreat Cranmer, making him dance attendance at the door, "'mong boys, grooms and lackeys", and then summoning him to a kind of inquisition. The lord chancellor speaks for the prosecution, and accuses Cranmer:

> *Chan.* ... you, that best should teach us,
> Have misdemeaned yourself, and not a little,
> Toward the King first, then his laws, in filling
> The whole realm, by your teaching and your chaplains' –
> For so we are informed – with new opinions,
> Diverse and dangerous, which are heresies,
> And, not reformed, may prove pernicious.
> *Gard.* Which reformation must be sudden too,
> My noble lords; for those that tame wild horses
> Pace 'em not in their hands to make 'em gentle,
> But stop their mouths with stubborn bits, and spur 'em
> Till they obey the manège. If we suffer,
> Out of our easiness and childish pity
> To one man's honour, this contagious sickness,
> Farewell all physic – and what follows then?
> Commotions, uproars – with a general taint
> Of the whole state, as of late days our neighbours,
> The upper Germany, can dearly witness,
> Yet freshly pitied in our memories.

(5.2.47–65)

The "heresies" in question are of course the Protestant ideas of the Reformation, here condemned by conservative Catholics as those of a "new sect", of which Cranmer is not only a member, a "sectary", but an evangelical champion of Protestant "teaching". These "new opinions" are dangerous, as witness the recent civil conflicts in Germany (referring to the Peasants' War of 1524–25). Ironically the words "reformation" and "reformed" are here appropriated (from John Foxe) by opponents of the Protestant Reformation, who are actually advocating Counter-

Reformation and the suppression of the Protestant "heresy". The king then enters to rescue Cranmer from his ordeal at the hands of the bishop and the Catholic lords. Gardiner salutes Henry as a king "most religious", who "makes the church/The chief aim of his honour". Henry demonstrates the truth hidden in this flattery by favouring the Protestant Cranmer, an "honest man", against his opponents, and selecting him for the duty of baptizing the baby Elizabeth:

> … my lord of Canterbury,
> I have a suit which you must not deny me:
> That is a fair young maid that yet wants baptism –
> You must be godfather, and answer for her.

(5.2.193–96)

Henry will use the rite of baptism to signal the advent of his new dynastic hopes, and to gather the faithful into a unified community. All members of the society can benefit from this social cohesion, and Henry expects his subjects to lay aside their differences, whether doctrinal or political, in the interests of the common good.

> *King.* I long
> To have this young one made a Christian.
> As I have made ye one, lords, one remain –
> So I grow stronger, you more honour gain.

(5.3.211–14)

The language of community – "one remain" – anachronistically echoes the baptism rite in *The Book of Common Prayer*, which reorients the ritual from a sacrament of cleansing to a reception of the child into Christian community:

We receive this Child into the congregation of Christ's flock…
Seeing now dearly beloved Brethren that these children be regenerate
and grafted into the body of Christ's congregation…

And this is where the play ends, with Archbishop Cranmer's speech proclaiming Elizabeth as England's new hope:

> This royal infant – heaven still move about her –
> Though in her cradle, yet now promises
> Upon this land a thousand thousand blessings
> Which time shall bring to ripeness. She shall be –
> But few now living can behold that goodness –
> A pattern to all princes living with her,
> And all that shall succeed… Truth shall nurse her,
> Holy and heavenly thoughts still counsel her.
> She shall be loved and feared. Her own shall bless her;
> Her foes shake like a field of beaten corn,
> And hang their heads with sorrow. Good grows with her.
> In her days every man shall eat in safety
> Under his own vine what he plants, and sing
> The merry songs of peace to all his neighbours.
> *God shall be truly known*, and those about her
> From her shall read the perfect ways of honour,
> And by those claim their greatness, not by blood.

(5.4.17–37, my italics)

Queen Elizabeth will prove an ideal monarch, "the pattern to all princes". Her reign will restore a golden age, though the allusion here is not classical but biblical, to the visions of an earthly paradise to be found in 1 and 2 Kings, Isaiah, and especially Micah 4:4: "they shall sit every man under his vine, and under his fig tree". The queen's power will be sustained by divine knowledge, since she will be counselled by "holy and heavenly thoughts", and "truth will nurse her". Above all, in her reign, "God will be truly known", which goes so far as to imply that previously such knowledge had been obscured by the religious teaching of the time. This revelation will persist into the age in which the play itself is written and performed: Elizabeth will, Cranmer prophesies, be succeeded by another monarch "as great in admiration as herself" – James I. Only in the reigns of Elizabeth and her Protestant successor James will the divine favour bestowed on England, and on her monarchs, become fully revealed, and open to common understanding.

§

There were very good reasons for creating such a play at the time *Henry VIII* was written and produced. The play can be dated with unusual precision as written before 20 June 1613, since on that day the Globe Theatre burned down during a performance of *Henry VIII*. In February 1613 James I's daughter Princess Elizabeth was married to Prince Frederick, the Elector Palatine. The union was widely heralded as signalling an alliance between two strong Protestant states, and a defence against the power of the papacy "to check the Popish pride". Dramatist Thomas Heywood celebrated Frederick as "the religious Protestants' protector". There were also in 1613 some concerns over national security: rumours that the pope was preparing a new Armada to invade the country from without, and that Catholic resistance within the realm, suppressed after the Gunpowder Plot of 1605, was raising its head again. Coastal defences were stepped up, and weapons confiscated from Catholic houses. There could be no more constructive and appropriate accompaniment to this national context than a play showing the downfall of the last great Catholic statesman of England, the ascension of Cranmer, and the birth of Queen Elizabeth, whose name was revived in the person of James's daughter. Although Shakespeare's company, the King's Men, certainly performed a number of Shakespeare's plays before Frederick and Elizabeth, *Henry VIII* is not mentioned; it seems difficult to separate it from the context of national celebration, expected social harmony, and required religious unity. Past and present are paralleled, and history spills over into the present. When Garter King of Arms in the play blesses the young Elizabeth, daughter of Henry VIII, at her baptism in 1533, his benediction would have applied just as fittingly to the princess Elizabeth, daughter of James I, whose marriage in 1613 was currently being celebrated:

> Heaven, from thy endless goodness, send prosperous life, long and ever happy, to the high and mighty princess of England, Elizabeth.

(5.4.1–3)

Chapter Four

"King of snow": *Richard II*

Shakespeare wrote ten plays on English history. Two groups of four, known as the first and second tetralogies, deal respectively with the Wars of the Roses (1454–87), and with the historical period between 1399 and 1415, from the deposition of Richard II to Henry V's victory at Agincourt. The first tetralogy – that is, the one written first – consists of the three parts of *Henry VI* and *Richard III*, and was written in the early 1590s. The second tetralogy contains *Richard II*, *Henry IV Parts One and Two*, and *Henry V*, and was written 1595–99. Thus the first series Shakespeare wrote deals with the later historical period. In addition, and independent of these two series, there is an early play, *King John* (1596), and the late play, *Henry VIII* (1613), discussed in the previous chapter.

The next two chapters address the two plays that book-end the "second tetralogy": *Richard II* (1595) and *Henry V* (1599). I will argue that these two plays not only narrate and interpret a significant period of English history, but also address some key issues of religious faith and doctrine. The two eponymous kings are presented as case studies in how to, and how not to, rule, while the two plays comment indirectly on questions of politics and religion both in the time of their historical setting, and in the reign of Queen Elizabeth.

§

Richard II begins with a political crisis. Like all mediaeval kings ruling a still largely feudal society, Richard is dependent on the loyalty of his nobles to maintain his power for him. In a feudal society the king is relatively weak, since it is the nobles who have their own private armies of retainers, while there is no national army loyal to the monarch. We are introduced to a king who is clearly arrogant and high-handed in his relationship with his nobility. The opening action of the play shows a high-ranking member of the aristocracy, Henry Bolingbroke, later Henry IV, now Earl of Hereford, son to the duke of Lancaster, John of Gaunt, challenging another noble, Thomas Mowbray, Duke of Norfolk, on charges of embezzlement and treachery. These allegations remain vague and insubstantial, since Bolingbroke's real case against Mowbray is that he was responsible for the murder of Bolingbroke's uncle, Thomas of Woodstock, Duke of Gloucester.

> He did plot the Duke of Gloucester's death…
> Sluiced out his innocent soul through streams of blood;
> Which blood, like sacrificing Abel's, cries
> To me for justice and rough chastisement…

(1.1.100–106)

Here again Shakespeare employs the biblical story of Cain and Abel to represent a kind of founding crime; one which violates all social bonds and generates a future cycle of violence and recrimination. Mowbray admits he was involved in the murder. But the sub-text here, only implied in the play though clear in the historical sources, is that the king himself was responsible for Gloucester's death. Bolingbroke is not defending the king against a traitor, but attacking the king through his accomplice, Mowbray. Thus Richard himself is here accused of being a

Cain, a guilty shedder of his own family's blood. His complaint harnesses the poetry of the Bible – "the voice of thy brother's blood crieth unto me, from the earth" – and thus mines to a deeper level of feeling and experience than the context of political wrangling that contains it, signalling that this play will be about something larger than political questions of authority and obedience, civil conflict, and social order.

The characters are acting out a legal process, though one that belongs to this particular type of feudal society, and is hardly recognizable as such from the point of view of modern criminal law. The two protagonists "appeal" one another of treason, and Bolingbroke challenges Mowbray to a duel. The language they share is a chivalric discourse of honour and aggression, rather than a language of legal procedure:

> *Bol.* Pale trembling coward, there I throw my gage…
> *Mow.* I'll answer thee in any fair degree
> Or chivalrous design of knightly trial…

(1.1.69–81)

So the two men are agreeing to engage in an ordeal by battle, the ancient chivalric code based on the principle that might is right, and the outcome of a fight tantamount to justice. The ordeal seems an absurdity to modern judicial process, though it survives as a pattern of poetic justice in popular fiction and film.

The trial by battle is elaborately set up at Coventry in Act 1, Scene 3, deploying the full splendour of mediaeval chivalric ceremony. Both the combatants declare their absolute belief in the justice of their cause, and place their trust in God, who will adjudicate the combat and decide the winner.

> *Mow.* … by the grace of God and this mine arm
> To prove him, in defending of myself,

A traitor to my God, my king, and me.
And as I truly fight, defend me heaven!....
Bol. Harry of Hereford, Lancaster, and Derby
Am I, who ready here do stand in arms,
To prove by God's grace and my body's valour
In lists on Thomas Mowbray, Duke of Norfolk,
That he is a traitor...

(1.3.22–39)

In the previous scene, John of Gaunt, Duke of Lancaster, in conversation with the widow of his murdered brother Thomas of Gloucester, also places his faith in the outcome of the combat. He admits that he is powerless to revenge his brother's death, as the murderer is the king: "for God's substitute,/His deputy anointed in his sight,/Hath caus'd his death" (1.3.37–39). Hence "God's is the quarrel", and only God can decide.

But the big event proves to be an anti-climax. Just as the knights are about to engage, the king uses his authority to stop the fight, and banishes both men from England. The two nobles have entrusted their fates to God in the trial by combat, but Richard usurps that divine power, pre-empts the ultimate decision, and imposes his own will. From the point of view of a more centralized monarchy like that of Elizabeth, and a more secular perception of the machinery of political power, this would seem an eminently sensible solution. But in the England of 1398 it proves to be a catastrophic error of judgment, which ultimately brings down both Richard and the Plantagenet dynasty whose direct line he completed. As we shall see, when Bolingbroke's son Henry V puts his sovereignty to the test in the Battle of Agincourt, he is very careful to ensure that the outcome is understood as determined only by God.

As a ruler Richard is portrayed critically, as tyrannous and capricious, subject to the influence of "flatterers" and "favourites", unable to command the loyalty of the aristocracy upon whose power his authority depends. This is the context of John of Gaunt's famous "this England" speech, offered to the king as a dire warning of the folly of his irresponsibility, and the dangers of his neglect:

> This royal throne of kings, this sceptred isle,
> This earth of majesty, this seat of Mars,
> This other Eden, demi-paradise,
> This fortress built by nature for herself
> Against infection and the hand of war,
> This happy breed of men, this little world,
> This precious stone set in the silver sea,
> Which serves it in the office of a wall,
> Or as a moat defensive to a house
> Against the envy of less happier lands;
> This blessed plot, this earth, this realm, this England…

(2.1.40–50)

Gaunt's vision is of an England that once existed, though it is now virtually ruined by Richard's mismanagement: "That England, that was wont to conquer others/Hath made a shameful conquest of itself" (2.1.65–66). Other than the image of England as an earthly paradise, an "other Eden", and the notion of the kingdom as "blessed", there is no religious language in this celebration that praises the nation rather for its traditions of royalty, its natural defences, and its sovereignty. Gaunt reserves his religious register for that section of the English population he really admires – the chivalric and crusading aristocracy:

> This nurse, this teeming womb of royal kings,
> Feared by their breed and famous by their birth,

> Renowned for their deeds as far from home
> For Christian service and true chivalry
> As is the sepulchre, in stubborn Jewry,
> Of the world's ransom, blessed Mary's Son...

(2.1.51–56)

Gaunt's admiration and loyalty are directed toward the past, and toward warrior monarchs like Richard I, who led their nobles on crusades to the Holy Land: king and people united in a common religious cause, serving God in "Christian service and true chivalry". Despite the present tense of Gaunt's national celebration of "this England", that ideal realm has already vanished into the past. England is now hopelessly degraded and compromised, and the king is little more than a "landlord".

§

As soon as Gaunt dies Richard makes his second crucial mistake: that of expropriating Lancaster's estates and disinheriting his banished son, against the protests of the other nobles. Richard shows himself determined to rule with a kind of absolute power, independent of his subjects' wishes: "Think what you will," he says as he overrides their objections. He departs for Ireland, leaving the inevitable baronial rebellion to organize itself behind his back. In his absence Bolingbroke returns, illegally, from banishment with an army, ostensibly to claim back his dukedom, but actually (or very quickly) beginning to harbour designs on the throne itself, since he rapidly establishes a power-base, and has the king's "favourites" executed.

Up to this point Richard has presented a most unflattering image of himself as king: arrogant and high-handed, capricious and tyrannical. He banishes Bolingbroke and Mowbray in order to conceal his own guilt in the murder of Woodstock, as well as to get rid of an obvious trouble-maker. He seizes Gaunt's

84

assets without any respect to traditions of inheritance, thereby alienating all his barons. He behaves recklessly, insensitively, apparently sufficiently confident in the power of his own authority to override the interests and opinions of his subjects. In practice he is setting aside the very principle of inheritance upon which his own authority as king rests. But on his return from Ireland, to face a full-blown rebellion with Bolingbroke as an obvious rival contender for the throne (they were both grandsons of Edward III), Richard becomes a different kind of king, and begins, belatedly, to speak a language of divine kingship:

> Not all the water in the rough rude sea
> Can wash the balm from an anointed king.
> The breath of worldly men cannot depose
> The deputy elected by the Lord.
> For every man that Bolingbroke hath pressed
> To lift shrewd steel against our golden crown,
> God for his Richard hath in heavenly pay
> A glorious angel. Then if angels fight,
> Weak men must fall; for heaven still guards the right.

(3.2.50–8)

A king cannot be deposed, Richard affirms, since he has been appointed and anointed by God, who will protect the king's authority, if necessary by divine intervention. Richard is thinking here entirely on a metaphysical plane, paying no attention to the actual conditions of power-politics in the real world around him. His supporters, the bishop of Carlisle and Aumerle, make a distinction between the divine "Power" invoked by Richard, and the sort of "power" being deployed by Bolingbroke, the power of armies and strategic alliances. The two kinds of power must operate in unison to be effective.

Car. Fear not, my lord. That power that made you king
Hath power to keep you king in spite of all.
The means that heavens yield must be embraced
And not neglected…
Aum. He means, my lord, that we are too remiss,
Whilst Bolingbroke, through our security,
Grows strong and great in substance and in friends.

(3.2.27–31)

Within the mediaeval context of their dramatic life, the distinction these characters make is simply between the ultimate will of God, and the worldly means by which that will becomes implemented on earth. For a more modern sensibility such as Shakespeare's, the distinction allows for a sceptical, secular understanding of power, which in reality seems to operate quite independently of divine will. God is on the side with the biggest battalions. This doesn't necessarily point to the conclusion that there is no God, and no divine control over human affairs; only that his will is not so easy to perceive, and that the king who relies simply on his own divinely appointed authority is likely to be overthrown by the man who understands the mechanisms of power. Or to put it another way, there is a fundamental divergence in the play between Richard's fundamentalist literalism, and Bolingbroke's grasp of the gaps between words and what they signify. When Richard names the signs of power, he clearly for a time believes that they carry the force of real power, and become indistinguishable. The king's anointed person is untouchable: a crown is real authority; a sceptre is the equivalent of an army. Bolingbroke understands that this is not so: that signs can be detached from the objects they refer to, and replaced with other signs, as kingly power can in practice be transferred from one man to another. Richard's approach to ruling is absolutist and literal; Bolingbroke's contingent and representational. Their respective approaches parallel the controversies between Catholic and Protestant views of signification, especially around the Eucharist. In the former, the sacramental elements were very much not signs pointing to some external referent, but were in themselves referent, sign and signifier; in the latter the elements became significant, not substantial.

Richard clearly is guilty of the neglect of which Aumerle accuses him. News immediately reaches him that a Welsh army expected to support the king has failed to materialize – dispersed, or defected to Bolingbroke. This loss throws Richard into a mood of tragic despair: no army of angels will appear to substitute for the real army that has deserted him; his destiny draws near – "time hath set a blot upon my pride". The sudden collapse of Richard's confidence in his own authority is remarkable, and seems to indicate a character all too willing to embrace defeat. He literally converts in an instant from a proud, despotic ruler to a martyr, a sacrificial victim who immediately begins to compare himself to Christ, betrayed by Judas. The prospect of defeat releases in him a morbid preoccupation with death as the ultimate destiny of all human hopes:

> No matter where. Of comfort no man speak.
> Let's talk of graves, of worms and epitaphs,
> Make dust our paper, and with rainy eyes
> Write sorrow on the bosom of the earth.
> Let's choose executors and talk of wills –
> And yet not so, for what can we bequeath
> Save our deposed bodies to the ground?

(3.2.140–6)

Richard has no heir, and therefore nothing to bequeath except his own body, which is that of a king "deposed", but also by implication the body of Christ "deposed" from the cross. The ceremony of worldly power proves to be no more than a superficial show, as hollow as the grave, as empty of meaning as a "little scene" in the theatre:

> … within the hollow crown
> That rounds the mortal temples of a king
> Keeps Death his court and there the antic sits,
> Scoffing his state and grinning at his pomp,
> Allowing him a breath, a little scene,
> To monarchize, be feared, and kill with looks,
> Infusing him with self and vain conceit,
> As if this flesh which walls about our life
> Were brass impregnable; and humoured thus,
> Comes at the last, and with a little pin
> Bores through his castle wall; and farewell, king!

(3.2.156–66)

The awareness of mortality, of the fragility of human life, comes to Richard only in defeat, as he acquiesces to the inevitability of his own overthrow. His encounter with suffering humanity compares to the human suffering of Christ, but if he is indeed only a man, then his sacrifice cannot possibly claim the same kind of meaning. A man can be betrayed, crucified, deposed, but he cannot save the world. Suddenly conscious of his own vulnerability as an ordinary man, without the protection of kingly power, he looks within himself and finds only weakness, the natural condition of humanity. The castle's defensive walls can readily be breached; the body's protective wall of flesh easily pierced by a "little pin". In an anticipation of the journey of self-discovery undertaken by King Lear, beneath the gorgeous trappings of royal majesty Richard encounters essential humanity in the form of an exposed and vulnerable creature.

Cover your heads, and mock not flesh and blood
With solemn reverence. Throw away respect,
Tradition, form, and ceremonious duty,
For you have but mistook me all this while.
I live with bread, like you; feel want,
Taste grief, need friends. Subjected thus,
How can you say to me I am a king?

(3.2.167–73)

If the king can be "subjected" to these common wants and needs
– hunger, loss, grief, loneliness – then he is himself a "subject"
and no longer king, no longer semi-divine, no longer deserving
of "solemn reverence". As when the altars are stripped in the
church on Maundy Thursday, so all formal ceremony must now
be discarded: "tradition, form and ceremonious duty" must be
cast away. Richard has encountered and adopted the iconoclastic
spirit of the Reformation. "Christ's Gospel," affirms *The Book of
Common Prayer*, "is not a Ceremonial law (as much of Moses'
law was,) but it is a religion to serve God, not in bondage of the
figure or shadow, but in the freedom of spirit…"

§

Nonetheless Richard continues to assert his authority through
the fantasy of divine kingship, divorced from any actual basis
of power, indicating that he is still "in bondage of the figure",
trapped within his own symbolism. "Show us the hand of God,"
he says to Northumberland,

That hath dismissed us from our stewardship.
For well we know no hand of blood and bone
Can grip the sacred handle of our sceptre,
Unless he do profane, steal, or usurp.

(3.3.76–79)

"The hand of God" is a key phrase in Calvin's *Institutes* (1.16.9): that which becomes visible and appears to be the consequence of human action is in reality the visible manifestation of divine power. Despite what Richard says, hands of blood and bone have already seized his sceptre, and Richard knows it. At first sight he appears here to be reneging on his earlier mood of philosophical resignation. But he is no longer defending his own kingship: he is instead threatening those who depose him with a kind of curse comparable to the plagues of Egypt, with a future in which the political repercussions of their actions will fall upon them with the terrible punishment of divine vengeance:

> Yet know my master, God omnipotent,
> Is mustering in his clouds on our behalf
> Armies of pestilence; and they shall strike
> Your children yet unborn and unbegot,
> That lift your vassal hands against my head
> And threat the glory of my precious crown.

(3.3.84–89)

Like the Egyptians who enslaved the children of Israel, Richard's enemies will be afflicted with plagues. This warning of a providential curse upon the usurper is at this point ignored, but it is something that succeeding generations have to struggle with, right up to the accession of the Tudors. Later the bishop of Carlisle formulates this idea of a curse which became a cornerstone of the "Tudor Myth", the ideology justifying the accession of Henry VII as finally uniting a nation divided by civil wars for almost a century following the deposition of Richard II. The king, "the figure of God's majesty", cannot, according to the bishop, be fairly judged and condemned by his own subjects. If Bolingbroke is crowned king, that will make him a traitor and a usurper, and bring divine displeasure down on the nation and its people:

And, if you crown him, let me prophesy
The blood of English shall manure the ground,
And future ages groan for this foul act.
Peace shall go sleep with Turks and infidels,
And in this seat of peace tumultuous wars
Shall kin with kin and kind with kind confound.
Disorder, horror, fear, and mutiny
Shall here inhabit, and this land be called
The field of Golgotha and dead men's skulls.
O, if you rear this house against this house
It will the woefullest division prove
That ever fell upon this cursed earth!

(4.1.127–38)

The deposition of the anointed king, prophesies Carlisle, will provoke civil war, as indeed it does, a consequence dramatized in Shakespeare's *Henry IV* plays, and already previously followed through in his plays on the Wars of the Roses. England will become like Golgotha, the site of Christ's execution, the "place of the skull", a land of death and desolation. Here the bishop endorses Richard's presentation of himself as a kind of proxy for Jesus, betrayed and unjustly put to death, while the predicted calamities echo Old Testament prophecies of the destruction of Israel, and their recapitulation by Jesus himself in the New Testament.

§

The dismantling of Richard's ceremonial kingship is finally accomplished in the "deposition scene", in which he voluntarily resigns the crown, though in such a studied and formal manner that the ritual paradoxically produces a new kind of theatrical or even quasi-religious power, which clearly unnerves his opponents. Slowly and deliberately, Richard reverses all the ceremonial gestures of coronation – crowning, the assumption of majesty; the donation of the sceptre, symbol of power; anointing with the oil of chrism, which confers on the king the divine authority of his office. The ritualization of what might otherwise be perceived simply as a transfer of power from a weak to a strong ruler, a "regime change", draws attention to the idea of sacred kingship which is here being simultaneously promoted and denied:

> Now mark me how I will undo myself.
> I give this heavy weight from off my head,
> And this unwieldy sceptre from my hand,
> The pride of kingly sway from out my heart.
> With mine own tears I wash away my balm...

(4.1.193–97)

By employing a ceremonial, even liturgical language of speech and gestures, Richard is able to harness the sacerdotal charisma of kingship in a compelling display, and to make it clear to both the theatre audience and the other characters that political power that lacks divine authorization is simply *force majeure*, which may or may not be supported and sustained by justice. To "unking" the king – an oxymoron – is an act of treachery and betrayal, and since Richard has voluntarily resigned the crown, he recognizes that he himself ranks as a traitor along with the others:

> Mine eyes are full of tears; I cannot see.
> And yet salt water blinds them not so much
> But they can see a sort of traitors here.
> Nay, if I turn mine eyes upon myself
> I find myself a traitor with the rest,
> For I have given here my soul's consent
> T'undeck the pompous body of a king,

> Made glory base and sovereignty a slave,
> Proud majesty a subject, state a peasant.

(4.1.234–42)

Richard has colluded in a process of diminishment, much larger in its implications than the simple replacement of one king by another. No future king will be able to rely on an authority flowing simply from "pomp", the external display of majesty. Royal glory is now debased, and majesty subjected. Political power is exposed as a cruel and impersonal mechanism by means of which the strong can compel the weak to obey their will.

A little earlier in the scene Richard identifies himself with Christ, betrayed by Judas, and even compares the ritual he is stage-managing to a church service:

> Yet I well remember
> The favours of these men. Were they not mine?
> Did they not sometime cry, "All hail!" to me?
> So Judas did to Christ. But He in twelve
> Found truth in all but one; I, in twelve thousand, none.
> God save the King! Will no man say "Amen"?
> Am I both priest and clerk? Well then, Amen.

(4.1.158–64)

His hearers are so completely silenced by the theatrical and liturgical potency of his self-presentation, that not one will return the expected response to "God save the king". "Am I both priest and clerk?" Richard asks. Does he have to declaim both the office and the responses for himself? Is he the only one left in the virtual church of his imagination in which this ritual is taking place: the only one left who believes in kingship as a divine office?

Richard's imagining of the alternatives open to him once he has shed his kingly power are also explicitly religious in form. He fantasizes about becoming an anchorite, a hermit, free to travel along the sacred roads of mediaeval pilgrimage (roads that had already in Shakespeare's time been largely closed by the Reformation).

> I'll give my jewels for a set of beads,
> My gorgeous palace for a hermitage,
> My gay apparel for an almsman's gown,
> My figured goblets for a dish of wood,
> My sceptre for a palmer's walking staff,
> My subjects for a pair of carved saints...

(3.3.146–51)

All these properties of mediaeval Catholic piety belong to the pre-Reformation past. This is one of many religious quests – pilgrimages, crusades – that are fantasized in Shakespeare's history plays, but are never to take place. This is not what happens to deposed kings, as Richard well knows from his rehearsal of their innumerable and depressingly similar "sad stories". Like Sir Walter Raleigh in the Tower, awaiting execution and writing the poem "His Pilgrimage" – "Give me my scallop-shell of quiet/My staff of faith to walk upon" – the true goal of such a fantasy pilgrimage is invariably death. Imprisoned in Pontefract ("Pomfret") Castle, Richard enjoys at last a temporary period of suspension in which he is able to exercise his mind on spiritual meditations. All his thoughts are unhappy, and so they jumble divine and secular considerations, setting "the faith against the faith".

> ... no thought is contented. The better sort,
> As thoughts of things divine, are intermixed

With scruples, and do set the faith itself
Against the faith, as thus: "Come, little ones",
And then again,
"It is as hard to come as for a camel
To thread the postern of a small needle's eye."

(5.5.11–17)

One moment the message of the Gospels seems to be an inclusive, universal salvation, as when Jesus welcomes all children in Matthew 19:14: "Jesus said, Suffer little children, and forbid them not to come unto me: for of such is the kingdom of heaven." At other times the message is much more exclusive, as when Jesus suggests that the wealthy are virtually barred from the kingdom of God: "It is easier for a camel to go through the eye of a needle, than for a rich man to enter into the kingdom of God" (Mark 10:25). This apparent inequality could be interpreted as Calvinist election, but Richard sees it as doctrinal conflict and self-defeating paradox, "the faith against the faith". Either all are saved, or only a few. Where does Richard himself fit into this self-contradictory scheme of salvation?

Finally Richard is murdered in his prison cell by a knight, Sir Piers of Exton, acting not on Henry's direct order, but taking his cue from the new king's obvious wish to be rid of his predecessor. Presented with Richard's corpse, Henry experiences a violent revulsion against the deed he had clearly wished for and implicitly advocated: "though I did wish him dead,/I hate the murderer, love him murdered" (5.6.39–40). The pervasive allusion to Cain's slaying of Abel, which Henry himself had used to accuse Mowbray in the play's first scene, now returns to haunt him. Exton is identified with the biblical assassin, and must become a wanderer on the face of the earth, dwelling in darkness and the shadow of death, bearing Cain's curse:

> With Cain go wander through the shades of night,
> And never show thy head by day nor light.

(5.6.43–44)

But of course the guilt of Richard's murder cannot so easily be transposed to a scapegoat, and Henry knows it.

> Lords, I protest my soul is full of woe
> That blood should sprinkle me to make me grow.

(5.6.45–46)

The new regime is rooted in violence and injustice, founded as it is on the deposition and sordid assassination of the rightful king. Political authority clearly can be, indeed often is, established and maintained on the basis of such founding violence; after all Cain went on to father a dynasty, including a son, Enoch, who built the first city. But the new ruler acknowledges that spilt blood is not the best nurturer of legitimate authority. And so Henry vows to embark on a crusade in the hope of redeeming his kingship from its originating contamination of violence and injustice. It is a promise the king often recalls, especially on his deathbed. But it is not a promise he is ever destined to keep.

> I'll make a voyage to the Holy Land
> To wash this blood off from my guilty hand.

(5.6.49–50)

The day of crusades is past. A different kind of foreign expedition will be required to cleanse the kingdom – and this task falls to the succeeding king, Henry V.

CHAPTER FIVE

"MIRROR OF ALL CHRISTIAN KINGS": *HENRY V*

The two parts of *Henry IV* mediate between *Richard II* and *Henry V*, chronicling the first Lancastrian king's unquiet reign (it is Henry IV who speaks the famous line "uneasy lies the head that wears the crown"), and the civil conflicts that divide the kingdom following the deposition and murder of King Richard. Throughout these two plays we also observe the growth and development of Henry's son Prince Hal, destined to become, on his father's death, Henry V.

§

At the beginning of *Henry IV Part One* the prince has a terrible reputation for drinking, whoring, frequenting taverns, and wasting his time with low-life companions, especially his vicious but charming mentor in depravity, Sir John Falstaff. But in a key soliloquy delivered early in the play, the prince reveals to the audience that he intends to become something very different from his reputation as a notorious dissolute:

> I know you all, and will awhile uphold
> The unyoked humour of your idleness.
> Yet herein will I imitate the sun,
> Who doth permit the base contagious clouds

To smother up his beauty from the world,
That when he please again to be himself,
Being wanted he may be more wondered at,
By breaking through the foul and ugly mists
Of vapours that did seem to strangle him.
If all the year were playing holidays,
To sport would be as tedious as to work;
But when they seldom come, they wished-for come,
And nothing pleaseth but rare accidents.
So when this loose behaviour I throw off
And pay the debt I never promised,
By how much better than my word I am,
By so much shall I falsify men's hopes,
And like bright metal on a sullen ground,
My reformation, glitt'ring o'er my fault,
Shall show more goodly and attract more eyes
Than that which hath no foil to set it off.
I'll so offend to make offence a skill,
Redeeming time when men think least I will.

(1.2.173–95)

Here Prince Hal promises a personal "reformation" that needs to be understood in both political and religious terms. On the one hand there is something Machiavellian about this carefully calculated programme of political advancement, which employs dissimulation and concealment to hide his real motives. On the other hand, the carnal vices to which Hal admits are exactly those condemned by Protestant reformers: idleness, irresponsible sport, perpetual holiday. Politics and religion meet here in a "Protestant work-ethic". In promising to "redeem the time", Hal is talking not only about his own hitherto wasted life, but about the need to redeem his dynasty, his kingdom, and his age.

His intention is eventually to put in the serious work needed to save his own soul, to purge the Lancastrian line of its taint of usurpation, and to rescue the realm from the providential curse of social division that afflicts it. He will prove a tireless labourer for the good of the commonwealth, and he will put everyone else to work as well. At the very inception of his character's development, then, the future Henry V must strike us as a Protestant reformer with a Calvinist streak.

By contrast his image of the converted self, shining like "bright metal on a sullen ground", "show[ing]" more impressively, and "attract[ing] more eyes" inevitably recalls Richard II's investment in superficial display, and the splendid pageantry of Catholic worship:

> And like bright metal on a sullen ground,
> My reformation, glitt'ring o'er my fault,
> Shall show more goodly and attract more eyes
> Than that which hath no foil to set it off.

(1.2.190–94)

It is true that when he emerges from the "sullen ground" of his prodigal youth as a reformed character, Henry intends to dazzle spectators with a sudden accession of brightness that will eclipse his former faults. But his "reformation" will have to be a real transformation, not merely a concealment of sin beneath a façade of superficial brightness, which is how Protestant reformers thought of Catholic iconography. Later (1.2.270–3) Henry implicitly compares himself with the Prodigal Son in St Luke's parable, suggesting both that his errancy has been authentic and that his return will be more pleasing to the Father than the stolid reliability of those who never strayed (see Luke 15:11–32).

At the end of *Henry IV Part Two* as the newly crowned Henry V, Henry follows through on this promise of personal and social reformation in his rejection of Falstaff:

> I know thee not, old man. Fall to thy prayers;
> How ill white hairs become a fool and jester!
> I have long dreamt of such a kind of man,
> So surfeit-swell'd, so old, and so profane;
> But being awake, I do despise my dream.
> Make less thy body hence, and more thy grace…
> Presume not that I am the thing I was,
> For God doth know, so shall the world perceive,
> That I have turned away my former self;
> So will I those that kept me company. …
> And as we hear you do reform yourselves,
> We will, according to your strengths and qualities,
> Give you advancement.

(5.5.45–68)

The Calvinist streak is again abundantly visible here, as Henry preaches to Falstaff the need for reformation of character ("reform yourselves"), the rejection of sin and the absolute imperative of "grace". Henry himself is born again: "I have turned away my former self", echoing St Paul's epistle to the Ephesians:

> *The truth is in Jesus,*
> *That is, that ye cast off, concerning the conversation in time*
> *past, that old man, which is corrupt through the deceivable lusts,*
> *And be renewed in the spirit of your mind,*
> *And put on the new man…*

(Ephesians 4:21–24)

Here Paul insists on the necessity of casting off "that old man" (renouncing one's former self), a phrase that could almost have suggested the turning away of Falstaff (Falstaff and his companions are referred to as "Ephesians of the old church" – that is the unregenerate sinners Paul was trying to convert – in *Henry IV, Part Two* [2.2.144]). "Presume not that I am the thing I was," Henry declares: he has already "turned away" the metaphorical "old man" of his previous dissolute life, and will now exile the actual "old man" Falstaff, the "tutor of [his] riots". He has followed St Paul, "put on the new man", embraced the spirit of conversion, and thoroughly reformed himself. The identification of sin, the corruptible body and "the old man" also recur in the baptismal rite in the 1559 *Book of Common Prayer*:

> ... *humbly we beseech thee to grant that [this child] being dead unto sin, and living unto righteousness, and being buried with Christ in his death, may crucify the old man, and utterly abolish the whole body of sin...*

This reformation is publicly recognized and acknowledged by the archbishop of Canterbury at the beginning of *Henry V*:

> The breath no sooner left his father's body,
> But that his wildness, mortified in him,
> Seemed to die too. Yea, at that very moment
> Consideration, like an angel came
> And whipped the offending Adam out of him,
> Leaving his body as a paradise,
> T'envelop and contain celestial spirits.
> Never was such a sudden scholar made;
> Never came reformation in a flood
> With such a heady currance scouring faults...

(1.1.26–35)

The language here is again that of St Paul, especially the epistle to the Romans, which develops the idea of humanity as the "first Adam", and Christ as the second. In Henry the old sinful Adam is put to death, and paradise restored. But it is also the language of the baptism service in Shakespeare's *Book of Common Prayer*, the same rite by which he himself and all his children were baptized:

> *O merciful God, grant that the old Adam in these children may be so buried, that the new man may be raised up in them. Amen.*
> *Grant that all carnal affections may die in them, and that all things belonging to the spirit may live and grow in them. Amen.*

The "offending Adam" is the disobedient patriarch who committed the original sin that has to be washed away by the waters of baptism. In Henry, Canterbury claims, original sin is removed by divine intervention precisely at the point that he succeeds to the crown.

The term "mortified" in the speech quoted above also occurs in the 1559 baptism service:

> *… as [Christ] died and rose again for us: so should we (which are Baptised) die from sin, and rise again unto righteousness, continually mortifying all our evil and corrupt affections…*

The rite of baptism seems to be in Henry's mind as well, when later he exhorts the clergy to advise him responsibly:

> For we will hear, note, and believe in heart
> That what you speak is in your conscience washed
> As pure as sin with baptism.

(1.2.30–32)

A certain scepticism about the validity of this "reformation", which seems too sudden and complete (given the prince's previous life of depravity), flows as an ironic undercurrent through this conversation. But perhaps the prince's reformation has been developing quietly beneath the surface? Or perhaps he was simulating rather than truly embracing a vicious life? "It must be so," says Canterbury:

> … for miracles are ceased,
> And therefore we must needs admit the means
> How things are perfected.

(1.1.67–69)

By the time of the play's composition Protestant Christianity had identified belief in the continued occurrences of religious miracles as a typically Catholic dogma. Shakespeare leaves us in no doubt that if Henry is to carry through this personal "reformation" into a reform of his kingdom, then it will have to be by means of a genuine process of social transformation. God does not automatically defend the legitimate authority, unless that authority defends itself.

§

The first act of *Henry V* makes clear that a whole range of motives – economic, political, strategic – underlies the decision to invade France, and that some of these are highly questionable. But the background to Henry's decision is the "unquiet reign" of his father, and what he sees as the imperative to unify the kingdom. It was his father Henry IV's ambition to lead the nation on a crusade to the Holy Land, though this never happened. Henry V will lead his people on an expedition of foreign conquest, not to Palestine, but to France, and though this invasion and occupation is not a crusade, it serves the same purpose: that of uniting the nation against a common enemy. However devious and Machiavellian may be the motives, the people of England, according to the Chorus, enthusiastically embrace the opportunity, and are "following the mirror of all Christian kings".

Throughout the play Henry presents himself as a particular kind of "Christian king": one who is not despotic, has self-control, speaks with unvarnished "plainness", and places a supreme value on the imputed gift of divine grace:

> We are no tyrant, but a Christian king,
> Unto whose grace our passion is as subject
> As are our wretches fettered in our prisons...

(1.2.241–43)

Having determined to invade France to recover his title, Henry assigns the outcome solely to God's will:

> ... this lies all within the will of God,
> To whom I do appeal...

(1.2.289–90)

The historical Henry V is reported to have said at this point that he would proceed "by the aid of God, in whom is my whole trust and confidence" (Holinshed 3.547). Shakespeare's Henry is more Protestant than his real-life Catholic counterpart, since he does not assume that God will "aid" him, but as a petitioner merely lodges his request ("appeal") with the authority of the divine will. This displacement of glory from king to God recurs throughout the play, often articulated in a very Protestant language, as when the Chorus describes Henry as formally renouncing any personal triumph:

he forbids it,
Being free from vainness and self-glorious pride,
Giving full trophy, signal, and ostent
Quite from himself, to God.

(5.0.19–22)

Before the decisive Battle of Agincourt, Henry admits to the French herald that he is at a significant military disadvantage, his army weak and exhausted. He tells Montjoy he has resigned himself and his cause to God:

For, to say the sooth –
Though 'tis no wisdom to confess so much
Unto an enemy of craft and vantage –
My people are with sickness much enfeebled,
My numbers lessened, and those few I have
Almost no better than so many French…
Yet, forgive me, God,
That I do brag thus. This your air of France
Hath blown that vice in me. I must repent.
Go, therefore, tell thy master here I am;
My ransom is this frail and worthless trunk,
My army but a weak and sickly guard.
Yet, God before, tell him we will come on,
Though France himself and such another neighbour
Stand in our way.

(3.6.128–44)

Henry sounds Lutheran or even Calvinist when he renounces boasting and vainglory. And the conception of humanity as nothing more than a "frail and worthless trunk" chimes with this Protestant declaration. Henry pursues this theology in depth in the great Act 4, Scene 1, the night before Agincourt, where he wanders through his camp disguised, converses with some of his soldiers and finally reveals his own mind in a powerful soliloquy.

In discussion with the common soldiers Henry affirms that "Every subject's duty is the King's; but every subject's soul is his own" (4.1.176–77). Each person is responsible for his or her own salvation, unmediated by priest or ritual. No external authority, neither church nor state, can guarantee salvation. We see how Henry combines his insight into human frailty and worthlessness, a Protestant theology of individual salvation, and a sense of accountability towards his soldiers and his subjects in general (which he denies when speaking to them, but admits in soliloquy). He says to Bates that the king's "ceremonies laid by, in his nakedness he appears but a man" (4.1.105–106). As we have seen, "ceremony" was a key term in the English Reformation's assault on Catholic forms of worship. "Ceremony" denoted both the number of sacraments, the majority of which seemed to Protestants non-scriptural and unnecessary to salvation, and the visual theatre, the "scenic apparatus" of traditional Catholic worship. The second (1552) *Book of Common Prayer* introduced a preface entitled "Of Ceremonies: why some be abolished and some retained" (reprinted in subsequent editions, including that of 1559).

Some at the first were of godly intent and purpose devised, and yet at length, turned to vanity and superstition: some entered into the Church, by indiscreet devotion, and such a zeal as was without knowledge; and for because they were winked at in the beginning, they grew daily to more and more abuses, which not only for their unprofitableness, but also because they have much blinded the people, and obscured the glory of God, are worthy to be cut away, and clean rejected...

§

Henry's denunciation of what he calls the "idol ceremony" can
be read firmly within this Protestant context:

> What infinite heartsease
> Must kings neglect that private men enjoy?
> And what have kings, that privates have not too,
> Save ceremony, save general ceremony?
> And what art thou, thou idol ceremony?
> What kind of god art thou, that suffer'st more
> Of mortal griefs than do thy worshippers?
> What are thy rents? what are thy comings in?
> O ceremony, show me but thy worth.
> What is thy soul of adoration?
> Art thou aught else but place, degree and form,
> Creating awe and fear in other men?…
> No, thou proud dream
> That play'st so subtly with a king's repose;
> I am a king that find thee, and I know
> 'Tis not the balm, the sceptre, and the ball,
> The sword, the mace, the crown imperial,
> The intertissued robe of gold and pearl,
> The farced title running fore the king,
> The throne he sits on, nor the tide of pomp
> That beats upon the high shore of this world –
> No, not all these, thrice-gorgeous ceremony,
> Not all these, laid in bed majestical,
> Can sleep so soundly as the wretched slave
> Who with a body filled and vacant mind
> Gets him to rest, crammed with distressful bread…
> And follows so the ever-running year
> With profitable labour to his grave.

And, but for ceremony such a wretch,
Winding up days with toil and nights with sleep,
Had the fore-hand and vantage of a king.

(4.1.218–29; 239–52; 258–62)

At one level Henry is talking about the pomp and ceremony of kingship – "the balm, the sceptre, and the ball/The sword, the mace, the crown imperial" – and apprehending that such "ceremony" provides no protection to a monarch who has exposed himself, as he has, to the same risks, dangers, and anxieties as his soldiers. But his language is also religious – "idol", "god", "adoration" – and closely parallels the language in which Protestants reprimanded the "dark and dumb" ceremonies of Catholic worship as mere superstitions designed to keep subjects in "awe and fear". Cranmer called the Catholic sacrament an "idol". Henry sets a much higher value on the "profitable labour" of the ordinary working man than on what *The Book of Common Prayer* calls the "unprofitable" pageant of "ceremony". All this Protestant rhetoric does not stop the king from following the example of his historical original in establishing chantries for the relief of King Richard's soul (4.1.290–303), or from invoking the saints Crispin and Crispian. But he seems to understand that none of these "good works" will be efficacious in winning the battle. For that he needs God's help.

Henry's great speech of exhortation before the battle has been compared to a sermon or homily, since it includes an invocation of the shoemaker saints, Crispin and Crispian, and rededicates their day to be held in remembrance of the hoped-for English victory. The speech is less about inspiring the troops with the spirit of Catholic martyrs, and more about transforming a traditional French saint's day into an anniversary of English national triumph.

This day is called the Feast of Crispian.
He that outlives this day, and comes safe home
Will stand a-tiptoe when the day is named
And rouse him at the name of Crispian.
He that shall see this day, and live t'old age
Will yearly on the vigil feast his neighbours
And say "Tomorrow is Saint Crispian."
Then will he strip his sleeve and show his scars
And say "These wounds I had on Crispin's day."
Old men forget; yet all shall be forgot,
But he'll remember, with advantages
What feats he did that day. Then shall our names,
Familiar in his mouth as household words –
Harry the King, Bedford and Exeter,
Warwick and Talbot, Salisbury and Gloucester,
Be in their flowing cups freshly remembered.
This story shall the good man teach his son,
And Crispin Crispian shall ne'er go by,
From this day to the ending of the world
But we in it shall be remembered…
We few, we happy few, we band of brothers.
For he today that sheds his blood with me
Shall be my brother; be he ne'er so vile,
This day shall gentle his condition.
And gentlemen in England now abed
Shall think themselves accursed they were not here,
And hold their manhoods cheap whiles any speaks
That fought with us upon Saint Crispin's day.

(4.3.40–59; 60–67)

In future the annual "vigil" for Crispin and Crispianus will
memorialize not the wounds of the executed martyrs, but

wounds acquired in the course of achieving an English victory. The litany will not enumerate the names of saints, but the names of the heroic English: "Harry the King, Bedford and Exeter,/Warwick and Talbot, Salisbury and Gloucester" (4.3.53–55) shall all be "freshly remembered". The "flowing cups" of commemoration inevitably suggest Holy Communion, though the "host", the consecrated body of Christ, will be replaced by a verbal sacrament in which the "host" (4.3.34) of heroic English soldiers will be to each participant "familiar in his mouth" (4.3.52). This narrative will be repeated until the end of the world, like the narrative of the Passion incorporated into the celebration of the Eucharist in *The Book of Common Prayer* – "a perpetual memory of that his precious death, until his coming again". Like the Passion, Agincourt will seal itself into sacramental remembrance by the shedding of blood: "For he today that sheds his blood with me/Shall be my brother" (4.3.61–62). This image of the royal blood commingling with that of his followers indicates that Henry is not offering himself as a martyr-leader to replace the Catholic saints, but rather insisting that the whole English army can collectively achieve such status by their willingness to shed blood for their country.

§

After the victory of Agincourt, Henry repeatedly insists that all the glory should be ascribed to God, and none to the human beings who actually fought and won the battle.

> O God, thy arm was here!
> And not to us, but to thy arm alone,
> Ascribe we all.

(4.8.106–108)

"Take it, God," he says, "For it is none but thine" (4.8.111–12).
He even provides for any transgression of this doctrine to be
treated as a capital crime:

> And be it death proclaimèd through our host
> To boast of this or take that praise from God
> Which is his only.

(4.8.108–10)

Towards the close of the play (and, it should be admitted, in
a light-hearted context, Henry's wooing of the French princess
Katherine) the king states that he has a "saving faith" within
him: that is, a faith sufficient to salvation (5.2.191). Henry V
is, in every sense, a reformed character, and he has brought
reformation to his kingdom. The "star of England", the "mirror
of all Christian kings", is a Protestant national monarch very
much like Henry VIII or Queen Elizabeth I.

Chapter Six

"A PATTERN IN HIMSELF": *MEASURE FOR MEASURE*

Measure for Measure (1603) is Shakespeare's most explicitly religious play. Its action concerns questions of law and morality, sin and punishment, repentance and absolution, all played out within a nominally Christian, and largely Roman Catholic, context. Its setting is Vienna, a city that had become Protestant, but was re-Catholicized during the Counter-Reformation, and from 1556 was both the seat of the Holy Roman Emperor, and a strong base for the Jesuits (Edmund Campion taught in Vienna). The world of the play is distinctively Roman Catholic: a world of monasteries and convents, of friars and nuns, of canon law and auricular confession. The Catholic culture of the play is represented for the most part objectively, without animus or hostility, but a pervasive Protestant sensibility is also brought to bear on the spiritual and ethical problems with which the play deals.

§

The title itself alludes to Scripture, as the duke makes explicit at the close of the play:

> The very mercy of the law cries out
> Most audible, even from his proper tongue,

> "An Angelo for Claudio, death for death"
> Haste still pays haste, and leisure answers leisure;
> Like doth quit like, and measure still for measure.

(5.1.399–403)

The duke's deputy, Angelo, who has simultaneously imposed the strict letter of the law on a fornicator (Claudio), attempted to seduce his, Claudio's, sister Isabella, a novice, and covertly ordered the execution of the brother he has corruptly promised to save, deserves the equitable justice of the Mosaic law:

Breach for breach, eye for eye, tooth for tooth: such a blemish as he hath made in any, such shall be repaid to him.

(Leviticus 24:20)

But the duke finds "an apt remission" in himself, and applies the spirit of the New Testament:

Ye have heard that it hath been said, An eye for an eye, and a tooth for a tooth. But I say unto you, Resist not evil: but whosoever shall smite thee on thy right cheek, turn to him the other also.

(Matthew 5:38–39)

Judge not, that ye be not judged. For with what judgment ye judge, ye shall be judged, and with what measure ye mete, it shall be measured unto you again.

(Matthew 7:1–2)

Claudio, in prison and expecting to be executed for his offence, invokes the same religious authority in an echo of St Paul's epistle to the Romans. The secular authorities have the power to impose "measure for measure", however arbitrary such rough justice might appear:

Thus can the demigod Authority
Make us pay down for our offence, by weight,
The bonds of heaven. On whom it will, it will;
On whom it will not, so; yet still 'tis just.

(1.2.100–104)

The allusion is to Romans 9:

*For he saith to Moses, I will have mercy on him, to whom I will
show mercy: and will have compassion on him, on who I will have
compassion.*

(Romans 9:15)

But the duke, as the true secular authority, does not attempt to
impose such symmetrical justice on God's behalf. Under his
aegis crimes are pardoned, sins absolved, forfeits "remitted".
The moral of the play is not after all "measure for measure", an
eye for an eye, and a tooth for a tooth, but the forgiveness of sins
by the intervention of grace (a word used twenty-two times in
the play). "*It is* not in him that willeth, nor in him that runneth,
but in God that showeth mercy" (Romans 9:16).

While the duke throughout most of the play disguises
himself as a friar, wearing a cowl, haunting monasteries and
hearing confessions, his substitute Angelo is "a man of stricture
and firm abstinence", an embodiment of the popular idea of
Puritanism:

Lord Angelo is precise,
Stands at a guard with envy, scarce confesses
That his blood flows, or that his appetite
Is more to bread than stone.

(1.3.50–53)

"Precise" was a term commonly used of "Puritans", those Protestant reformers who thought it possible to "purify" the Church of England from within (as distinct from separatists). Archbishop Matthew Parker coined both "Puritan" and "precisian" in 1564 as terms of abuse levelled at Protestants dissatisfied with the Elizabethan religious settlement. Thus "Puritan" referred to a cause of ecclesiastical reform, not to an ascetic way of life, though the two quickly became confused, as when Shakespeare in *Twelfth Night* refers to the killjoy Malvolio as "a kind of Puritan". Or as the dissolute Lucio unsympathetically but accurately characterizes Angelo later in *Measure for Measure*:

> ... a man whose blood
> Is very snow-broth; one who never feels
> The wanton stings and motions of the sense,
> But doth rebate and blunt his natural edge
> With profits of the mind, study, and fast.

(1.4.56–60)

"Profits of the mind" parallels Henry V's "profitable labour". Such extreme asceticism is not to be trusted, since it denies the natural sinfulness of humanity: the blood must flow, hunger must be satisfied, however pure and sinless a man may profess himself to be. Sanctification is an illusion. Entrusting his authority to Angelo, the duke employs images that allude to the controversy between *sola fide* and good works:

> *Duke:* Angelo,
> There is a kind of character in thy life,
> That to th'observer doth thy history
> Fully unfold. Thyself and thy belongings

Are not thine own so proper as to waste
Thyself upon thy virtues, they on thee.
Heaven doth with us as we with torches do,
Not light them for themselves, for if our virtues
Did not go forth of us, 'twere all alike
As if we had them not. Spirits are not finely touched
But to fine issues; nor Nature never lends
The smallest scruple of her excellence
But, like a thrifty goddess, she determines
Herself the glory of a creditor,
Both thanks and use.

(1.1.26–40)

At the outset then the duke opens up a key theme of the play,
the consistency or discrepancy between external appearance and
inner virtue. The word "character" meant primarily "distinctive
handwriting", a signifier that should (but doesn't necessarily) reveal
("fully unfold") what we now mean by character, the authentic
personality, the inner man. The external "character" of Angelo's life
suggests he would be incorruptible, a reliable bearer of political and
judicial power. But what the duke goes on to say raises the possibility
of a division between being and seeming. If Angelo were to practise
his virtue in solitude, the result would be a wasteful self-consumption.
"Our virtues" have to "go forth of us", make an impact, have
some discernible effect upon the world, or we can't really be sure
that they exist at all. We could easily read this as a Catholic duke
recommending to a "precise" Protestant a combination of faith and
good works as necessary to human salvation.

But if the duke and Angelo are counterpointed as Catholic
and Protestant respectively, Shakespeare does not assign them
appropriately different theologies. The main drift of the duke's
imagery in this speech in fact moves in a more Protestant

direction. Human beings are like torches, illuminated to shed light on objects around them. A "spirit" that doesn't produce some valuable effect on the world cannot really be as "finely touched" as it may appear to be. Nature does not lend virtue, but gives it away absolutely, as St Paul says in Romans of the free gift of God's grace. It is entirely up to the individual believer what he or she does with the gifts thus liberally and generously bestowed. Good works should flow from grace conferred. "Let your light so shine before men, that they may see your good works, and glorify your father which is in heaven" (Matthew 5:16, quoted from *The Book of Common Prayer*). There can be no suggestion here that good works might in themselves be valuable, or capable of purchasing redemption: Nature, like God, reserves "both thanks and use". If the spirit is faithful, then its practice will be virtuous. The tree is not dependent on its fruit. The effects of virtue show us only that faith exists, and that faith exists by the free gift of grace. And "Grace is grace," as one character ironically observes, "despite of all controversy".

The duke clearly suspects that Angelo, once dressed in the robes of authority, may well turn out to be something other than the man he seems. The action of the play is in one sense a test of "character":

> … Hence shall we see,
> If power change purpose, what our seemers be.

(1.3.54–55)

§

The duke is a kind of theocrat, a head of state with religious authority, who mediates between all parties and harmonizes all doctrines. The main protagonist opposing Angelo is Claudio's sister Isabella. She is a virgin about to enter the enclosed order of St Clare, having not yet taken her vows. As a virgin she may seem as sanctified as Lucio (perhaps mockingly) describes her:

> I hold you as a thing enskied and sainted.
> By your renouncement, an immortal spirit,
> And to be talked with in sincerity,
> As with a saint.

(1.4.33–36)

The rule of the order she contemplates joining is clearly a strict one: the nuns cannot speak with men, except in the presence of the prioress; and even when speaking, they may not reveal the face. Isabella represents a kind of Catholic fundamentalism that is in some ways equivalent to Angelo's religious extremism. Shakespeare poses against Isabella's rigid idealism a view of sexuality as natural, to be accepted and tolerated, here voiced by Lucio in telling her of Juliet's pregnancy:

> Your brother and his lover have embraced.
> As those that feed grow full, as blossoming time,
> That from the seedness the bare fallow brings
> To teeming foison, even so her plenteous womb
> Expresseth his full tilth and husbandry.

(1.4.39–43)

Pre-marital sex, and the unplanned pregnancy that follows, are as natural as eating (we recall that Angelo "scarce confesses… his appetite/Is more to bread than stone"), or the agricultural cycle of planting and harvest. The bucolic metaphor beautifully places sex within a context of natural creation. Shakespeare himself, of course, had to get married when Anne Hathaway became pregnant with his daughter Susanna.

Isabella and Angelo collide on the ground of Claudio's condemnation: Isabella is prompted by Lucio to intercede with Angelo on her brother's behalf.

> All hope is gone,
> Unless you have the grace by your fair prayer
> To soften Angelo…

(1.4.67–69)

Angelo has already rejected pleas for mercy from the old counsellor Escalus, on the basis that temptation, though universal, can be resisted, and that Angelo himself would willingly accept what he regards as a just punishment, were he to commit the same offence:

> *Ang.* 'Tis one thing to be tempted, Escalus,
> Another thing to fall.…
> You may not so extenuate his offence
> For I have had such faults; but rather tell me,
> When I that censure him, do so offend,
> Let mine own judgement pattern out my death,
> And nothing come in partial. Sir, he must die.

(2.1.17–18; 27–31)

Isabella advocates grace and mercy in a language that recalls passages from *Richard II* and *Henry V*, particularly in its devaluation of "ceremony":

> No ceremony that to great ones 'longs,
> Not the king's crown, nor the deputed sword,
> The marshal's truncheon, nor the judge's robe,
> Become them with one half so good a grace
> As mercy does.

If he had been as you and you as he,
You would have slipped like him, but he, like you,
Would not have been so stern.

(2.2.61–68)

Angelo, she protests, is deluded to imagine that humanity is anything other than sinful and culpable. "Proud man,/Dressed in a little brief authority" loses touch with fallen human nature, becoming "ignorant of what he's most assured", his "glassy essence" (2.2.120–23). The extraordinary phrase "glassy essence" has been extensively used by philosophers, who argue from it that the mind is not a mirror but a lens, able to see reality but unable to see itself. Hence man remains "ignorant of what he's most assured": unable, while he is seeing, to see the act of seeing itself. The context however is ethical, not epistemological. What Angelo is ignorant of is what human beings have reason to understand is their true nature: sinfulness. A true reflection will show sinful man as he is in reality, measured by the unachievable perfection of "heaven", more like an "angry ape" than a godlike "angel". When judging as a magistrate, Angelo should feel as a man, and recognize a common humanity in universal original sin:

Go to your bosom;
Knock there, and ask your heart what it doth know
That's like my brother's fault. If it confess
A natural guiltiness, such as is his,
Let it not sound a thought upon your tongue
Against my brother's life.

(2.2.139–44)

The "natural guiltiness" of original sin is a bond linking all humanity in a common condition. Mere self-awareness should be sufficient to permit Angelo to acknowledge the same vulnerability and culpability within himself, and to tolerate Claudio's transgression by remitting his sin and redeeming him from capital punishment. Angelo stands by the law as an absolute exigency, without possibility of mitigation. Isabella replies with the doctrine of the redemption:

> *Ang.* Your brother is a forfeit of the law,
> And you but waste your words.
> *Isa.* Alas, alas!
> Why, all the souls that were were forfeit once,
> And He that might the vantage best have took
> Found out the remedy. How would you be
> If He which is the top of judgment, should
> But judge you as you are? O, think on that,
> And mercy then will breathe within your lips,
> Like man new made.

(2.2.75–81)

The human, social law has its claim on Claudio, whose life is "forfeit", and Angelo sees no reason to modify that judgment. Isabella's appeal is to the fact that in Christian doctrine, the fall of man rendered every human soul "forfeit" to the law of God, guilty and liable to the punishment of eternal death. God could have left humanity to its fate, and saved himself a lot of trouble. But instead he "found out the remedy": gave his only Son, who was incarnate, made man, suffered on the cross, was buried, and rose again. In *Richard II*, Shakespeare calls Jesus "the world's ransom/Blessed Mary's son", the price paid to redeem the "forfeit". Angelo should surely follow the example of the supreme judge, who offered mercy and forgiveness, and remitted the penalty of the law. If Angelo were to reflect on how he himself should be judged, he would be compelled to acknowledge that mercy is the appropriate response to the common human condition of "natural guiltiness". Isabella's source texts are from Matthew and Ephesians:

Judge not, that ye be not judged. For with what judgment ye judge, ye shall be judged, and with what measure ye mete, it shall be measured unto you again.

(Matthew 7:1–3)

... cast off, concerning the conversation in time past, that old man, which is corrupt through the deceivable lusts,

And be renewed in the spirit of your mind,

And put on the new man, which after God is created unto righteousness, and true holiness.

Wherefore cast off lying, and speak every man truth unto his neighbour: for we are members one of another.

(Ephesians 4:22–25)

The gospel links merciful and empathetic judgment with equality of "measure", capturing both the Mosaic law and the play's title, while St Paul insists that the "new man" of the reborn spirit remains indissolubly a part of the human community: "we are members of one another". Here the Catholic Isabella is closer to Luther – "We will commit sins while we are here, for this life is not a place where justice resides" ("Letter to Melanchthon", 1521) – than she is to the Council of Trent – "For, in those who are born again, there is nothing that God hates... nothing whatever to retard their entrance into heaven" ("The Doctrine Concerning Original Sin").

"Hark how I'll bribe you," says Isabella to Angelo, seeming to broach the possibility of corruption. Certainly his reaction indicates that this is what he thinks she is doing: "How! bribe me?" But the "bribe" is not a commercial offer, but a reciprocity of prayer for pardon:

Isa. Ay, with such gifts that heaven shall share with
you....
Not with fond shekels of the tested gold,
Or stones whose rates are either rich or poor
As fancy values them; but with true prayers
That shall be up at heaven and enter there
Ere sun-rise, prayers from preserved souls,
From fasting maids whose minds are dedicate
To nothing temporal.

(2.2.152–58)

(The word "shekels" is unique to the Geneva Bible.) Isabella
specifically disclaims any notion that mercy can be bought, as
in the sale of indulgences. Only prayer, freely offered from a
contrite heart, can have any efficacy with God. So she will pray
for Angelo, in return for his pardoning her brother.

§

This is the point in the play where Angelo falls. His sudden
and precipitate collapse into a corrupt and compromised lust
for Isabella confirms everything the play has so far suggested
about authority and sin. The apparently saint-like holiness
of an ascetic man cannot be trusted, since man is inherently
sinful. Human beings are united in the commonality of "natural
guiltiness". Sexual desire will not be contained within the limits
imposed by a civic authority, however totalitarian and strictly
policed they may be.

Ang. From thee, even from thy virtue.
What's this, what's this? Is this her fault or mine?
The tempter or the tempted, who sins most, ha?
Not she; nor doth she tempt; but it is I
That, lying by the violet in the sun,

Do, as the carrion does, not as the flower,
Corrupt with virtuous season.

(2.2.166–72)

Initially disposed to blame Isabella for tempting him, Angelo quickly accepts that he cannot exculpate himself. Under exactly the same conditions one person will fall, another will stand fast. Responding to the effects of the same sunlight, the flower will blossom, the dead animal will rot. Like Calvin's distinction between "unconditional election" and "reprobation", under the same divine mercy some are saved, others damned (or, in later formulations, "passed by"). Angelo has certainly discovered his own "glassy essence", displaying an extraordinary self-knowledge:

Can it be
That modesty may more betray our sense
Than woman's lightness? Having waste ground enough,
Shall we desire to raze the sanctuary,
And pitch our evils there?

(2.2.172–76)

It is precisely Isabella's purity that stimulates Angelo's lust. The appropriate location of sexual misconduct is the "waste ground" of immorality – the brothel; Angelo's desire is to violate the temple of virtue, to "raze the sanctuary" and "pitch [his] evils there". Unmoved by female promiscuity, he is felled by the "modesty" of a virgin novice, provoked to fantasies of rape by the very innocence he desires to deflower.

What dost thou, or what art thou, Angelo?
Dost thou desire her foully for those things
That make her good?…

O cunning enemy, that, to catch a saint,
With saints dost bait thy hook! Most dangerous
Is that temptation that doth goad us on
To sin in loving virtue. Never could the strumpet,
With all her double vigour – art and nature –
Once stir my temper; but this virtuous maid
Subdues me quite. Ever till now,
When men were fond, I smiled, and wondered how.

(2.2.177–91)

Angelo's lust for Isabella is worlds away from the healthy, venial, mutual sexuality of Claudio and Juliet. His desire is a "foul" perversion of love, since it is also a desire to corrupt, to violate, to soil the cleanness of virtue. Angelo's love of goodness converts to sin as he contemplates the ravishment of goodness, despoiling what he loves, ruining God's creation to turn it into something more akin to his own natural depravity. With this insight comes a recognition of the truth Isabella used to persuade him: that he is no different from anyone else. Hitherto unable to understand why men can be "fond" enough to succumb to desire, now he knows. The torment of illicit desire and the propensity to fall from grace are the conditions of humanity.

§

While Angelo is enforcing the full penalty of the law, in a parallel scene the disguised duke is seen applying a completely different method that synthesizes both Catholic and Protestant approaches to sin and repentance. Though dressed as a friar, the duke speaks as a type of Christ himself: "I come to visit the afflicted spirits/Here in the prison," he says, echoing 1 Peter 3:19, which describes the crucified Christ entering the domains of death and hell. He meets the pregnant Juliet, and hears her confession, using the word "penitence", which suggests "penance", the formal name for the Roman Catholic sacrament. "I'll teach you how you shall arraign your conscience,/And try your penitence, if it be sound,/Or hollowly put on" (2.3.22–24). His auricular confession of Juliet follows the Catholic form of contrition, disclosure, and satisfaction. He asks if she repents of her sin, and requires her to confess it. Juliet answers as a good Catholic: "I do confess it and repent it, father." The duke ensures she is prepared to accept the consequences of her guilt, which she readily admits: "I do repent me, as it is an evil,/And take the shame with joy" (2.3.37–38). When contented with her answers, the duke gives a kind of perfunctory absolution: "There rest." Straying beyond the boundaries of the confessional, the duke also explores Juliet's sin as an instance of mutual guilt, in which Claudio is equally implicated, since the sin was "mutually committed". Here he shows that he shares common doctrinal ground with Isabella, and of course ultimately his role will be to impose mercy and forgiveness on all his subjects. His leave-taking merges a Protestant blessing later incorporated into *The Book of Common Prayer* ("The grace of our Lord Jesus Christ, and the love of God, and the communion of the Holy Ghost be with you all" [2 Corinthians 13:13]) with a Catholic, Latinate valediction: "Grace go with you, Benedicite!"

There follows the climactic scene (2.4) in which Angelo openly attempts to seduce Isabella. The scene opens with Angelo in soliloquy. Self-divided like Claudius in *Hamlet*, Angelo prays for deliverance, but finds himself too attached to his own desire and to its object to find any path to salvation.

> When I would pray and think, I think and pray
> To several subjects: heaven hath my empty words,
> Whilst my invention, hearing not my tongue,
> Anchors on Isabel; God in my mouth,

> As if I did but only chew his name,
> And in my heart the strong and swelling evil
> Of my conception.

(2.4.1–7)

The words of his prayer are emptied of significance. Angelo is like a man taking Holy Communion without faith, taking God into his mouth, but merely "chew[ing] his name". As Luther puts it:

> *This, now, is the entire Christian preparation for receiving this Sacrament worthily. For since this treasure is entirely presented in the words, it cannot be apprehended and appropriated in any other way than with the heart. For such a gift and eternal treasure cannot be seized with the fist.*

(The Large Catechism, 1529)

Again we find the attack on "ceremony", the kind of impressive superficial display designed to keep men in "awe", but which is nothing more than "false seeming".

> O place, O form,
> How often dost thou with thy case, thy habit,
> Wrench awe from fools and tie the wiser souls
> To thy false seeming! Blood, thou art blood:
> Let's write "good angel" on the devil's horn –
> 'Tis not the devil's crest.

(2.4.12–17)

The devil doesn't go around sporting his tell-tale horn; instead he wears the "crest" of a "good angel". Humanity stands between angel and devil, distinguished by what neither spiritual being possesses: the contaminated blood of original sin. "Blood, thou art blood": the basic physical property of human life is also the seat of "natural guiltiness".

> O heavens!
> Why does my blood thus muster to my heart,
> Making both it unable for itself,
> And dispossessing all my other parts
> Of necessary fitness?

(2.4.19–23)

Angelo is completely overwhelmed by his desire, articulated in the sensation of blood flowing to his heart as he sees Isabella. He offers her pardon for her brother in exchange for her body. She refuses, protesting that she cannot save her brother's life by imperilling her own immortal soul. Angelo retorts that her refusal makes her as cruel as the law:

> *Ang.* Were not you then as cruel as the sentence
> That you have slander'd so?

But Isabella again replies theologically:

> *Isa.* Ignominy in ransom and free pardon
> Are of two houses; lawful mercy
> Is nothing kin to foul redemption.

(2.4.112–14)

There is a world of difference, she says, between an ignominious bartering of money for ransom, and a free pardon. Equally Angelo cannot compare his proposed trade of female body for fraternal liberty as equivalent to "lawful mercy". As St Paul says in Romans 5:15, one of the main sources for the Protestant doctrine of justification by faith: "the gift is not so as is the offense". The offence of Adam, producing universal human death, was the offence of one man; but "the gift by grace, which is by one man Jesus Christ, hath abounded unto many" (Romans 5:15).

§

It is time to consider the overall role of the duke in *Measure for Measure*, since it is he whose manipulations drive the rest of the play's action, and it is he who is responsible for the final dramatic denouement, and the ultimate apportionment of justice. In fact the duke's influence over the dramatic narrative is such as to make him a kind of providential deity, arranging people and events into concord with poetic justice. He also runs the danger of being perceived as a Machiavellian manipulator, who moves people around like pieces on a chess board to ensure they fit his scheme of salvation.

Some of this is performed through the duke's disguise as a Roman Catholic friar (in fact he claims to be not only a friar but a papal legate), which enables him to move anonymously and with a kind of diplomatic privilege through the scenes of the play's action. He takes advantage of the "secret harbour" offered by a monastery, and to some limited degree takes a genuine brother, Friar Thomas, into his confidence. He hears confessions (such as that of Juliet, discussed above), speaks often of the confessional, and uses information gained from confession to further his plans. He persuades people to act in certain ways by exploiting the trust people repose in his assumed sacerdotal identity.

It is particularly important, then, that the audience or reader of the play should find the duke acceptable and congenial as the architect of the play's design, since many of the things he does seem questionable. He clearly has no intention of allowing Claudio to be executed, but persuades him to be ready for death, and advises Juliet that Claudio is to die. He tells Claudio that

Angelo's real intentions are honourable, a knowledge he claims to have gained from the confessional: "I am confessor to Angelo, and know this to be true". He then speaks to Isabella, tells her that he knows of Angelo's seductive and corrupt behaviour, and proposes as a catch-all solution to all the play's problems the "bed-trick" in which Mariana, previously betrothed to Angelo, will substitute for Isabella in Angelo's bed. Mariana is also persuaded by the duke to participate in the ruse. He happens, fortunately, to be in the prison when Angelo's treacherous order to execute Claudio arrives, and is able to reprieve him. At one stroke Isabella will be protected, Claudio saved from execution, Mariana's fortunes restored, and Angelo caught, exposed and trapped into marrying the woman he deserted. The final result will be justice: measure for measure. A formal poetic speech in rhyming couplets, delivered directly to the audience, shows the duke has a choric role outside the drama as well as an irenic role within it. He expounds the duties of a good ruler:

> Peace be with you.
> He who the sword of heaven will bear
> Should be as holy as severe;
> Pattern in himself to know,
> Grace to stand, and virtue go;
> More nor less to others paying
> Than by self-offences weighing.

(3.1.480–86)

The duke quotes Christ's own words from John 20:21, in a wording taken from the older Coverdale version, since both the Bishops' and the Geneva Bibles have "Peace be unto you". The ruler is God's deputy, bearing "the sword of heaven", and must therefore dispense justice with mercy as does God himself. He must fashion himself, by education and wisdom, into a "pattern", a model of wide and just governance. But he must also accept that human beings should judge their fellows in the way they would wish to be judged, as Jesus enjoins in the Sermon on the Mount: "Judge not, that ye be not judged. For with what judgment ye judge, ye shall be judged, and with what measure ye mete, it shall be measured unto you again" (Matthew 7:1–2).

When Angelo is unmasked, he recognizes the duke as a kind of quasi-divine authority:

> O my dread lord,
> I should be guiltier than my guiltiness
> To think I can be undiscernible,
> When I perceive your grace, like power divine,
> Hath looked upon my passes. Then, good prince,
> No longer session hold upon my shame,
> But let my trial be mine own confession.
> Immediate sentence then, and sequent death,
> Is all the grace I beg.

(5.1.358–66)

There are two distinct methods of dealing with sin and penitence at play here – the Catholic and the Protestant. The former relies on auricular confession, private absolution, and personal penance; the latter on public "general confession", collective absolution, and the public exhibition of shame. Angelo begs to be released from the Protestant requirement for public confession, the holding of a "session" on his shame, and to be permitted the privacy of trial and execution without open confession. The duke, however, restored to his own identity, demands public confession. In fact the word "confession" in the closing scenes begins to take on the more legalistic meaning of open confession, as in a criminal judicial process, and moves away from the traditional Catholic sense of confession to God through the intermediary of a priest. Finally the duke assigns judgment to all the principals on the basis of his theology of forgiveness and mercy. Claudio is forgiven when he "restores" Juliet by marrying her. Mariana is married to Angelo.

> She, Claudio, that you wrong'd, look you restore.
> Joy to you, Mariana! Love her, Angelo:
> I have confess'd her and I know her virtue.

(5.1.518–20)

And finally, in the most arbitrary gesture of all, the duke tells Isabella he will marry her.

> Dear Isabel,
> I have a motion much imports your good;
> Whereto if you'll a willing ear incline,
> What's mine is yours and what is yours is mine.

(5.1.527–30)

Given that Isabella had every intention of becoming a nun, has not been consulted at all on the subject of marriage, and has known the duke only in his disguise as a friar, this aspect of the duke's ceremony of reconciliation presents problems to many readers and spectators. But this resolution is a kind of poetic justice, not an attempt to establish fairness and equity that could be assessed sociologically. The duke is acting as both character and author, standing as proxy for the dramatist himself, whose job it is to arrange events in such a way as to convincingly resolve the "problems" of the play and to bring the comedy to a harmonious reconciliation. "This is all as true," as Isabella says, "as it is strange": the denouement is more about how a play should end in the theatre than it is about social conditions in early modern England, the professional opportunities of women religious, and the patriarchal imposition of marriage.

§

Presiding over the literal unmasking of Mariana, his own emergence from disguise and the metaphorical unveiling of Angelo's treachery and corruption, the duke conducts a ritual in which everything is brought into the open, and nothing remains hidden. He tests Isabella's capacity for forgiveness by lying about Claudio, letting her think him dead and inviting her to judge Angelo by the harsh justice of the Mosaic law:

> "An Angelo for Claudio, death for death"…
> Like doth quit like, and measure still for measure.

(5.1.401–403)

Isabella displays an extraordinary capacity for forgiveness in appealing on Angelo's behalf, arguing that he did not accomplish the crime he intended. Angelo is presented with the truth that others are capable of exercising undeserved forgiveness and mercy. At last Claudio is brought in hooded, then "unmuffled" on stage. All are forgiven, and the whole community unified by four marriages.

Thus the play is brought to its comedic resolution not by auricular confession and private penance, but by public humiliation and general absolution. The duke continually calls on the characters to "confess" in the open, and explicitly denies Angelo the option of private confession. Jestingly Lucio distinguishes between private and public confession:

> … if you handled her privately,
> she would sooner confess: perchance publicly
> she'll be shamed.

(5.1.272–73)

A PATTERN IN HIMSELF

But such open "shaming", conducted on stage before the theatre audience, common enough in the reformed church of Shakespeare's day (his own son-in-law Richard Quiney was sentenced to exactly such a ritual of open penance "in a white sheet (according to custom)" for fornication in 1616), is exactly what the duke's reformed Christianity requires. As in the exhortation to the people before Holy Communion in *The Book of Common Prayer*, all are required to attend, and to come together in godly community. No one is allowed to absent himself; all conflicts and differences should be laid aside; everyone must join in.

It is your duty to receive the Communion together, in the remembrance of his death as he himself commanded.

CHAPTER SEVEN

"THE QUALITY OF MERCY":
THE MERCHANT OF VENICE

This chapter discusses a play in which Shakespeare's own religion, Christianity, is located into a dramatic conflict against another, Judaism. As indicated earlier, Shakespeare, in common with other dramatists of his age, had a sophisticated understanding of historical belief systems, and was able, convincingly, to represent the spirituality of pre-Christian societies such as those of ancient Greece and Rome. *The Merchant of Venice* shows him engaging in a sustained comparison and contrast between two of the great world faiths, in the course of which, although Christianity is clearly promoted as the normative religion, Judaism is also treated with considerable understanding and even sympathy.

§

Venice was an obvious context in which to place a story about Christians and Jews. More than any other European city, Venice presented the model of a multicultural rather than monocultural society, one in which aliens such as Jews and Muslim Turks were accorded a proper place, partially segregated but protected by law. In Venice Jews could worship at their own synagogues and Muslims could pray to Allah without fear of inquisition or persecution. Venetian Jews lived in the Ghetto, a walled estate named after the island it was built on, a name that only later became synonymous with a space of urban deprivation. Although *The Merchant of Venice* does not mention the Jewish Ghetto, the institution was very well known, and its model of a segregated ethnic enclave clearly contributed to Venice's reputation for according to Jews an unusual degree of protection, as well as professional opportunity and social participation.

To some degree Venice offered the model of a more open, liberal, even modern society, which could not but be admired by progressive and enlightened minds of the day. Values such as tolerance, mutual respect for cultural difference, each man walking with his own god, seemed to many observers an admirable method of securing peaceful co-existence. Certainly Venice, for most of the time, remained relatively free from the common atrocities of anti-Semitic persecution, and the restless enmity between Christianity and Islam was fought out on the foreign rather than the domestic front.

But this early experiment in multicultural modernity was unusual, and to many observers disconcerting. This free mixing of "strangers" could seem colourful, or threatening. Such freedom was exciting, but also intimidating; it destabilized convention and undermined tradition. Borderlines became confused; distinctions blurred; things seemed to turn into something else. These paradoxes, typical of early modern views of Venice, feature strongly in Shakespeare's play.

§

The Jew Shylock is by profession a moneylender; he practises the "usury" that is the focus of such heated debate in the play, and was the subject of so much contemporary anxiety. Shylock lends money at interest on security of property or person. The objections brought against Shylock's practice from the Christians in the play are not objections to the practice of lending, or to the application of interest, or to charging a high rate of interest, for which Jews were extensively criticized (the word "excess" in the play simply means interest, not excessive interest). The moral objection to usury was an objection specifically against the charging of interest, as would be the case today, from the moment the loan is taken out. Christians had no quarrel with interest being added to the principal after the repayment date had passed (hence Antonio can reconcile himself to Shylock's "bond", which is not usurious in form). The difference is similar to that between a bank loan, on which you pay interest from the moment the agreement is signed, and borrowing on a credit card, where interest becomes payable only after the repayment date has passed. This distinction between different methods of borrowing and lending money was a key issue in the anti-usury propoganda of the early modern period, though it must seem to us today to turn on a very fine distinction, as both methods are widely used (though not of course in Islamic societies and communities, where banks operate so as to avoid usury).

Notwithstanding the mediaeval objections to usury, the growing capitalist economy could not manage without it. Everywhere in Renaissance Europe usury was condemned, but employed; detested and desired; damned from the pulpit and practised in the exchange. In Venice, possibly the most commercially advanced society in Europe, the problem was especially acute, since all forms of capital investment were needed to power the economy, and Venice's pragmatic and secularist rulers were reluctant to seal off any avenue of profitability. Thus various kinds of accommodation effected the adjustments necessary to make usury permissible.

The action of the play is triggered by the Christian merchant Antonio taking a loan from the Jewish moneylander Shylock, in order to assist his friend Bassanio. Antonio "only loves the world for him", and Bassanio admits his own immense indebtedness to his friend:

> To you, Antonio,
> I owe the most in money and in love…

(1.1.130–31)

Love and money are not incompatible bedfellows here, as they so often are in romance narratives. Both Antonio's willingness to lend or give, and Bassanio's sense of indebtedness, are expressions of love. There is also a religious dimension to this problem, opened up by Bassanio's critical description of himself as a "prodigal". Later Shylock insults Antonio by referring to him as a "prodigal", a waster and spendthrift. But in Christian terms "prodigal" cannot be read simply as a negative moralization, since the parable of the Prodigal Son in Luke justifies the prodigality of the child who wastes everything, rather than the unremarkable service of the child who loyally adheres to the family business.

> … you do me now more wrong
> In making question of my uttermost
> Than if you had made waste of all I have.

(1.1.155–57)

The parable is also of course a parallel to the Christian narrative of fall and redemption, through the costly self-sacrifice of the Saviour who gives everything via the *kenosis* of incarnation and Passion. In responding to Bassanio's needs, Antonio also speaks a language in which there is no division between love and money; purse and person; the offering of both body and goods:

> My purse, my person, my extremest means
> Lie all unlock'd to your occasions.

(1.1.138–39)

This extravagant openness of Christians to one another is sharply contrasted with Shylock's racial and religious exclusivity. Invited to dinner, Shylock indignantly refuses:

> Yes, to smell pork; to eat of the habitation which your prophet, the Nazarite, conjured the devil into. I will buy with you, sell with you, talk with you, walk with you, and so following; but I will not eat with you, drink with you, nor pray with you.

(1.3.28–32)

This manifesto of cultural difference prepares the way for Antonio's entrance, and for Shylock's first major speech – marked by a shift from prose to verse – in which he expresses the complex inter-relations of race, religion, and economics:

> *Shylock.* [*Aside*] How like a fawning publican he looks!
> I hate him for he is a Christian;
> But more for that in low simplicity
> He lends out money gratis, and brings down
> The rate of usance here with us in Venice.
> If I can catch him once upon the hip,
> I will feed fat the ancient grudge I bear him.
> He hates our sacred nation; and he rails,
> Even there where merchants most do congregate,
> On me, my bargains, and my well-won thrift,
> Which he calls interest. Cursed be my tribe
> If I forgive him!

(1.3.36–47)

Within the first few minutes of his stage presence, Shylock seems to have answered fully to all the anti-Semitic stereotypes of the Middle Ages, within which the Jews were conceived of as the murderers of Jesus; as infidels who stubbornly resisted the revelation of God in Christ; as miserly and anti-social, mercenary and treacherous (every Jew being a Judas); as evil, associated with the devil; and as capable of sacrilegious atrocity such as the abduction and ritual cannibalism of Christian children.

Shylock is preoccupied with money, and sees his relations to other people as consisting of financial transactions. He adopts an attitude of exclusiveness in his social and domestic life, shunning contact with those regarded by his religion as "unclean". He hates all Christians, and particularly Antonio, out of a mixture of cultural and economic animosities. The vindictive malice that comes to the surface on Antonio's entrance – "If I can catch him once upon the hip,/I will feed fat the ancient grudge I bear him" (1.3.421–22) – hints at the Jews' legendary reputation for cannibalism. The later comparison of human and animal meat in terms of relative market values –

> A pound of man's flesh taken from a man
> Is not so estimable, profitable neither,
> As flesh of muttons, beeves, or goats

(1.3.161–63)

– may also provoke the idea that both animals and men can be fed upon. When Shylock greets Antonio with "Your worship was the last man in our mouths", the expression raises the racist fantasy of Jewish cannibalism.

At the same time it is readily apparent that Shylock is being constituted by others into this archetypal figure, rather than forming that identity for himself; or rather that his dramatic role is shaped by an energy of resistance, rather than from an instinct of self-fashioning. He appears as the calculating usurer because that is the social function assigned to him by Bassanio, just as it was for the Jews of Venice – needed but officially despised by the Christian majority. The Christian does not show to advantage in this exchange. Bassanio is borrowing unscrupulously to satisfy his needs, but it is another, Antonio, who "shall become bound". Bassanio is trying to seal a commercial transaction between the Jewish usurer and a Christian merchant who very publicly takes a very high moral stand against usury.

In the light of this Christian unscrupulousness and hypocrisy, Shylock's obduracy can be interpreted as a legitimate resistance to the pressures exerted on him by men who would rather have nothing to do with him. When Shylock accepts Antonio's surety – "I think I may take his bond" – Bassanio responds indignantly: "Be assured you may." Shylock's reply: "I will be assured I may" (1.3.25) is masterly in its double entendre. Bassanio means "reassured", while Shylock is looking for what we would now call "insurance" – security of his capital. Is this Christian civility and enthusiasm pitted against Jewish calculation and malice, or the resistance of a persecuted minority to the high-handed hypocrisy of those who despise him and yet wish to make use of his services?

Shylock's hatred of Antonio is expressed in personal, economic, racial, and religious terms. Antonio is enveloped in a history of persecution and resistance. Antonio, claims Shylock, "hates our sacred nation", thus Shylock must hate him in return as a racial and religious duty: "Cursed be my tribe/If I forgive him." By referring to Jews as both "nation" and "tribe" Shylock identifies Christian animosity as ethnic hatred, but the tribe is also "sacred", so there is also a religious dimension to the reciprocal dislike. Shylock never shows any sign of a wish to "Judaize", to convert Gentiles to Judaism, but the Christians are unceasingly determined, both in jest and in earnest, to see Shylock undergo a forced conversion to Christianity.

Antonio does not of course restrict his hostility to verbal and physical abuse, but extends it into business dealing:

> He lends out money gratis and brings down
> The rate of usance here with us in Venice.

(1.3.39–40)

This strategic undermining of Shylock's legitimate business dealing, coupled with the physical and verbal violence Antonio publicly displays to Shylock, amounts to persecution. The public slights offered to the Jew may be aimed primarily at his business ("my moneys and my usances") but they take the form of personal insults and racial indignities ("spit upon my Jewish gabardine"). Shylock endures, for "sufferance is the badge of all our tribe". That "badge" is also worn as a mandatory signifier of Jewishness, initially in Venice a yellow circle, later the red hat or yellow turban. Far from denying these allegations of racial violence, Antonio threatens to continue his campaign of victimization.

> I am as like to call thee so again
> To spit on thee again, to spurn thee too.

(1.3.125–26)

Clearly, Shylock is looking out for an advantage over Antonio, but it is the latter who first introduces the idea of a financial transaction sealed in enmity rather than friendship:

> *Ant.* If thou wilt lend this money, lend it not
> As to thy friends – for when did friendship take
> A breed for barren metal of his friend?

(1.3.127–29)

The basis for Antonio's hatred is of course a moral distinction between different kinds of business dealing that in a modern capitalist economy would be very hard to separate. Shylock is a usurer: he lends money, on security of property or person, for a fixed term, with interest accruing from the date of the loan. In the event of forfeiture, the usurer keeps the property, or has legal purchase on the person (for example, by imprisonment for debt). Usury is clearly proscribed by passages in the Old Testament (Exodus and Leviticus), while Deuteronomy gives conditional permission: "Unto a stranger thou mayest lend upon usury, but thou shalt not lend upon usury unto thy brother" (23:20).

Thus in Jewish religious tradition the practice was forbidden between members of the Jewish faith, "brothers" within the tribe, but permitted to outsiders, Gentiles such as Christians. Christianity, being a universalizing religion in which, theoretically, all human beings are potentially "brothers", none necessarily strangers to God in Christ, received these Old Testament sources as total proscriptions on usury. This view was not however compatible with the fiscal needs of the growing capitalist economy, and in the course of the later sixteenth century, proscriptions against usury were relaxed, and it became accepted as a normal part of the business context. The debate on usury acted out in *The Merchant of Venice* however uses the traditional ethical and religious objections derived from Aristotle's *Ethics* and the Old Testament. When Antonio challenges Shylock to lend him money, not in friendship but in enmity, he echoes the Aristotelian objection to usury – that money being a "barren" thing should not breed more money – but also uses Shylock's own Judaic tradition against him: money should not be lent usuriously to a friend:

But lend it rather to thine enemy,
Who if he break, thou mayst with better face
Exact the penalty.

(1.3.130–32)

The business of the merchant is identified with universal friendship: that of the usurer with enmity. The former is regarded as disinterested and selfless, the latter grasping and selfish. The exchange of money for goods is seen as an activity that enriches not only the merchant, but the life of the community as a whole: fertilizing, enriching, fruitful; while the exchange of money for money is seen as sterile, wasteful, profitless. Shylock's defence of usury is couched in the form of a parable, using the story of Jacob and Laban's sheep (Genesis 30:25 – 31:16), which he reads as justifying commercial opportunism and the generation of an "excess" for the investor comparable to the interest the usurer takes from loans. Antonio rejects this argument, insisting that this was a "venture Jacob served for" – in other words a capitalist venture entailing risk, and subject to the arbitrament of chance or providence. Thus to Shylock, Jacob is the archetypal usurer; to Antonio he is an embryonic merchant capitalist. Both opponents read the same Scripture to produce different meanings justifying their respective commercial practices.

Antonio accepts Shylock's malicious bond, according to which a default on the debt will permit the Jew to take a pound of flesh from his body. Antonio's ships miscarry, and the debt is forfeit. Antonio's friends think the doge will inevitably set the contract aside, since it is so clearly unreasonable and disproportionate, but as Antonio points out, more is at stake here than his own life and liberty.

Sal. I am sure the Duke
Will never grant this forfeiture to hold.

Ant. The Duke cannot deny the course of law,
For the commodity that strangers have
With us in Venice, if it be denied,
Will much impeach the justice of the state,
Since that the trade and profit of the city
Consisteth of all nations.

(3.3.24–31)

This much-quoted passage serves as a judicial and commercial manifesto for Venice. The very basis of the city's survival, let alone its wealth and prosperity, is international trade. It is in the best interests of that international trade that members of other nations should be able to stay and practise their business safely and unhindered. If the doge were to show manifestly unfair preference to a Christian Venetian, then the justice of the state would be compromised, "impeached", revealed as a sham, and the Venetian economy would suffer in consequence. In terms of commercial law and contract, Shylock's position is, at this point in the play, unassailable and protected.

§

In the so-called "trial" scene (which is not technically a trial but a hearing to adjudge the validity of a contract), the doge invites Shylock to renounce his position as a "stranger", and to enter the moral consensus of Christian Venice:

And where thou now exacts the penalty –
Which is a pound of this poor merchant's flesh –
Thou wilt not only loose the forfeiture,
But touched with human gentleness and love,
Forgive a moiety of the principal,
Glancing an eye of pity on his losses,
That have of late so huddled on his back

Enough to press a royal merchant down
And pluck commiseration of his state
From brassy bosoms and rough hearts of flint,
From stubborn Turks and Tartars never trained
To offices of tender courtesy.
We all expect a gentle answer, Jew.

(4.1.21–33)

If Shylock could be touched by the universal values of "human gentleness and love", in observing the merchant's losses, he would be prepared not only to "loose the forfeiture", but even to cancel part of the original debt. Such compassionate empathy could be avoided only by those outside the Christian community, such as "stubborn Turks" – Muslims who have no instinct of Christian mercy and forgiveness – or pagan Tartars. As an inhabitant of Christian Venice, though a Jew, Shylock is offered participation in the benefits of its civilization. The corollary however is that Shylock's failure to concur must mark him out as an outsider, an infidel who, like the stubborn Turk, stands outside the Christian community of human gentleness and love. If Shylock is not merely pretending to pursue the suit to its inevitably fatal end, then his motives are clearly those of a hostile alien. The closing line of the doge's appeal contains a decisive pun: "We all expect a gentle answer, Jew."

"Gentle" is identified with "Gentile": the Jew is challenged to give not just a "merciful" but a *Christian* answer to the court's appeal.

Shylock avoids these ethical and religious arguments, and focuses exclusively on his bond. All he asks from the court is that his contract be upheld. This is Shylock's legal strategy, and it is an intelligent one, given the judicial context. Though he is proceeding on the basis of a law that offers universal protection,

Shylock does so from the position of a "stranger" rather than that of a citizen of Venice.

> I have possessed your Grace of what I purpose,
> And by our holy Sabbath have I sworn
> To have the due and forfeit of my bond.
> If you deny it, let the danger light
> Upon your charter and your city's freedom. …
> If you deny me, fie upon your law:
> There is no force in the decrees of Venice.
> I stand for judgement. Answer: shall I have it?

(4.1.34–38; 100–102)

Shylock speaks not of his own charter, city's freedom, or law, but of someone else's: your charter, the freedom of your city, your law. In other words Shylock is fully aware that this is not a simple application of the law to a contractual dispute, as it would be if the parties were fully equal Venetian citizens, but a test case which stretches the tolerance of the law to its full extent. An alien is claiming legal compensation from a Christian, so the demand for universal equality is launched from a position of cultural subjugation that in turn denies the equality claimed. Despite his continual iteration of the legal argument – the contract has been breached and the penalty is forfeit – this is a Jew seeking redress from a Christian court.

Antonio sees himself as having innocently come within reach of Shylock's diabolical snare ("his envy's reach") and, deprived of legal remedy, can only invoke the saintly virtues of patience and "quietness of spirit". In the course of the proceedings Shylock fulfils the classic role of the devilish, scheming, vindictive, bloodthirsty Jew. Though this is not a trial, Antonio stands on trial like Christ before Pilate, offering to lay down his life for a friend.

The legendary hard-heartedness of the Jews goes back to early Christian polemics in which they were characterized as stubborn, stiff-necked, refusing to accept the clear revelation of redemption in Christ – and of course manifestly cruel in handing Jesus over for torture and execution by the Romans. The trial scene locates Shylock firmly into this anti-Semitic tradition. Shylock rejects Christian salvation, even echoing the notorious blood-libel from the Gospel of Matthew 27:25 ("His blood *be* on us, and on our children") when he says, "My deeds upon my head!"

Shylock appears as the mercenary usurer, and as the betrayer, having tricked Antonio into the flesh-bond. He is associated, in jest and in earnest, with the devil, and his plan is not just to kill Antonio, but to ritualistically carve out his flesh in an obscene sacrament that recalls all the bizarre fantasies of Jews murdering Christian children to sprinkle their blood on the Passover bread. Shylock's cruelty is also a kind of forced conversion of Antonio to Judaism, a circumcision, taking literally what St Paul says about circumcising the heart rather than the body. Another version of the same idea from the possible source *The Orator* (1596) shows the Jew calculating his pound of flesh as the weight of the Christian's "privie members", "supposing that the same would altogether weigh a just pound". Circumcision by extension becomes castration as well as ritual murder. The language used by Shylock before the flesh-bond was sealed – "I will feed fat the ancient grudge I bear him" – now comes home in its interweaving of Old Testament language and imagery, the Mosaic law, vengeance, cannibalism, and ritual murder. Shylock the Jew is attempting to re-stage the crucifixion. His offences are the legendary crimes of his race: "His blood *be* on us, and on our children".

But of course Shylock is not a Jew from a mediaeval Passion play: he is the Jew of Venice.

Ant. The Duke cannot deny the course of law…

(3.3.26)

The apparent universality of Venetian justice in practice permits Shylock to stand for justice against the doge, the magnificoes, the entire Christian merchant community. In the course of the play's action Shylock is permitted to speak on behalf of what we would now regard as basic human rights and liberties: freedom of conscience and faith, the right to equality, dignity, and respect. He is placed in a position where he is able to expose Christian hypocrisy, and to confer dignity on Judaic culture and tradition, as when he speaks of the ring given to him by his betrothed, Leah. He pronounces a striking and unheard-of challenge to slavery, and upholds the cosmopolitan law of Venice that was so much admired at the time.

Shylock, then, has not made the trial into a clash of religions, but the Christian characters do. Each time Shylock is invited to join the Christian community and subscribe to its values, the discourse of invitation can be read as a reminder of his unequal cultural status. "How shalt thou hope for mercy," asks the duke, "rendering none?" Shylock's reply – "What judgement shall I dread, doing no wrong?" ("Why do I need mercy?") (4.1.87–88) – maintains the legal terminology, but seems to polarize Jewish law against Christian forgiveness, an opposition prominent in the later Christian Gospels, and thereby to accede to the transfer of the question from the realm of justice to that of belief. If mercy is conceived of as the dominant value of Christianity, then the duke is offering Shylock an unacceptable Christian solution to the problem.

Throughout the first half of the trial Shylock is continually assured that he is an equal in the eyes of the law, and is continually offered the opportunity of renouncing his suit and embracing the common values of Venetian civilization. But the offer is invariably couched in the language and imagery of the dominant Christian culture, which appears unwilling to embrace Shylock's otherness, and concede true quality to his alien status. He would be acceptable only as a Christianized Jew, in effect a "Marrano" who is prepared to renounce his race, religion, and beliefs along with his legal action against Antonio. Bassanio's newly wedded wife Portia, disguised as the lawyer Balthasar, seems to propose exactly the same solution, and to speak the same language: "Then must the Jew be merciful." She also seems to cite the opposition between Judaism and Christianity as religions respectively of justice and mercy.

> Therefore, Jew,
> Though justice be thy plea, consider this:
> That in the course of justice, none of us
> Should see salvation.

(4.1.193–96)

"Therefore by the works of the Law shall no flesh be justified in his sight" (Romans 3:20). If she is speaking here of Christian salvation, then the Jew can scarcely expect to participate in its benefits, and Portia would be proposing the same solution as the doge: that Shylock renounce his Jewish faith as well as giving up his suit.

But to use Portia's famous phrase, "Tarry a little." By using the phrase "none of us", Portia enfolds Shylock into a common Judaeo-Christian family. The language of justice, mercy, and salvation is only a Christian language because it was first of all a Jewish one. The Christian ideas of human depravity and grace invoked here by Portia, though extensively theorized by St Paul, are derived from the Old Testament. "Salvation" is just as important in Judaism as in Christianity, though it means something different.

The importance of mercy as a counterweight to inexorable justice pervades the Hebrew Scriptures as well as the Christian; one of the most insistent themes of the Old Testament is the continual cry of Israel to God for undeserved forgiveness.

Thus Portia's offer to Shylock is an ecumenical one, synthesizing the values of Judaism and Christianity into a common ethical language:

> *Portia.* The quality of mercy is not strained.
> It droppeth as the gentle rain from heaven
> Upon the place beneath. It is twice blest:
> It blesseth him that gives, and him that takes.
> 'Tis mightiest in the mightiest. It becomes
> The throned monarch better than his crown.
> His sceptre shows the force of temporal power,
> The attribute to awe and majesty,
> Wherein doth sit the dread and fear of kings;
> But mercy is above this sceptred sway.
> It is enthroned in the hearts of kings;
> It is an attribute to God himself,
> And earthly power doth then show likest God's
> When mercy seasons justice. Therefore, Jew,
> Though justice be thy plea, consider this:
> That in the course of justice none of us
> Should see salvation. We do pray for mercy,
> And that same prayer doth teach us all to render
> The deeds of mercy.

(4.1.180–96)

"My doctrine shall drop as the rain, *and* my speech shall still as the dew, as the shower upon the herbs, and as the great rain upon the grass" (Deuteronomy 32:2). The "mercy" invoked here is as Jewish as it is Christian. Portia appeals to a common Judaeo-

Christian intercession when she says: "We do pray for mercy,/ And that same prayer doth teach us all to render/The deeds of mercy." The Paternoster, or Lord's Prayer, was of course based on Jewish prayers such as the Kaddish and Shema, and Portia's words here have an exact counterpart in the apocryphal book of Sirach:

> *One man beareth hatred against another, and doth he seek pardon from the Lord? He sheweth no mercy to a man, which is like himself: and doth he ask forgiveness of his own sins?*

Ecclesiasticus 28:3–4

So this great speech on the quality of mercy, so often read as a Christian manifesto to challenge Jewish legalism, draws also on Deuteronomy and Ecclesiasticus, on *Hebrew* canonical and non-canonical Scriptures, where God's mercy "drops as the rain", "distils as the dew" (Deuteronomy 32:2; see also Ecclesiasticus 35:20). It is the *Jewish* concept of *rachamim*, compassion, she is celebrating, as much as the Christian concept of mercy. Shylock is not after all, as the trial reveals, equal before the tribunal of Venetian law, but he could be considered equal in terms of a shared religious inheritance.

§

Portia's speech takes us to the very heart of the play, and to the centre of the dramatic action. This is the point of no return, in which Shylock genuinely has the opportunity to put a stop to his suit, draw back, and agree to the court's terms. He has a real choice, because the solution proposed draws on his own religious and cultural traditions as well as those of his Christian opponents. At this point Shylock has the option of releasing his captive, and thereby showing more magnanimity than the slave-owning Venetians, who have no intention of manumitting their purchased slaves. He could renounce his claim to the forfeited loan, and thereby prove that money is not of supreme importance to him. He could emerge victorious from the legal process, enriched by the compensation Bassanio offers, and show himself morally superior to his enemy Antonio, by returning mercy for hatred. All this could be achieved without any need to renounce his faith or yield up his right to be treated equally by Venetian commercial law. Shylock could leave the courtroom as a victor. Nothing would protect him from a resurgence of ethnic hatred, but his position in Venice, and the protection Venice is obliged to afford him, would be more, rather than less, secure as a consequence of that moral victory.

Once Shylock goes past this point, he has lost the game. He could remain "the Jew of Venice", but he prefers to lapse back into a demonized identity as the Jew of Matthew's Gospel: "My deeds upon my head!" (4.1.201) ("His blood *be* on us, and on our children" [Matthew 27:25]).

This invocation of the notorious blood-libel is usually understood as Shylock reverting to type, or revealing that ingrained Jewish enmity that has never been very far from the surface in his speech and behaviour. But given the context, we can see this as Shylock choosing to assimilate to the atavistic demonic identity rather than assume that of the liberal modern citizen offered by Portia. Shylock has the opportunity to seize control of the action and to reverse its story of inveterate Jewish enmity pitted against Christian hatred. But he passes up that opportunity, and Portia has no choice but to proceed to give him the "law", the "justice", he asks for.

Portia leads Shylock almost to the point of Antonio's death, with her assurance that his suit is legally unassailable, and then with her injunction to pause – "Tarry a little" – produces a devastating dramatic reversal, which sets the action spinning off in a completely opposite direction. The law still gives Shylock the right to exact his penalty, but other statutes render the exaction of the penalty a criminal offence. These laws, unlike the law protecting the cosmopolitan freedom of commercial exchange, are designed to protect the Venetian citizen against the hostile actions of racial and cultural outsiders:

> Take then thy bond, take thou thy pound of flesh.
> But in the cutting it, if thou dost shed
> One drop of Christian blood, thy lands and goods
> Are, by the laws of Venice confiscate
> Unto the state of Venice.

(4.1.304–308)

The subsequent directive to cut off no more than "a just pound" seems to be part of the same law protecting Christian flesh against the non-Christian enemy. To subvert the law that treats all men equally, Portia invokes a law designed explicitly to treat them unequally. If the situation were reversed, the Jew would not by the same law be protected against the Christian. Finally, Portia reveals her bottom-line defence of Antonio, which is a conspiracy law targeted directly at the outsider:

> It is enacted in the laws of Venice,
> If it be proved against an alien
> That by direct or indirect attempts
> He seek the life of any citizen,
> The party 'gainst the which he doth contrive
> Shall seize one half his goods; the other half
> Comes to the privy coffer of the state,
> And the offender's life lies in the mercy
> Of the Duke only, 'gainst all other voice –
> In which predicament I say thou stand'st,
> For it appears by manifest proceeding

That indirectly, and directly too,
Thou hast contrived against the very life
Of the defendant, and thou hast incurred
The danger formerly by me rehearsed.

(4.1.343–57)

The "trial" thus begins with a deadlock of competing economic interests, in which there is no rational appeal beyond the validity of contract, and in which the protection afforded to contract by Venetian law binds the judicial authorities in a helpless subjection to the most literal legalism. The doge appeals to Shylock on the basis of a universal morality, where the dominant values are mercy and forgiveness, and offers Shylock the opportunity of incorporation into a harmonized political economy where Jews would rationally forfeit their legal rights in the interests of the public good, and into a Christian ethical world of reciprocal forgiveness and mutual sympathy.

Portia offers Shylock an entirely different solution, by drawing on the intertwined traditions of Judaism and Christianity, and inviting Shylock to acknowledge that what Jews and Christians have in common can transcend the accidents of their mutual opposition. Even though, as the denouement of the trial demonstrates, Portia is fully capable from the outset of exposing the true criminality of Shylock's proceeding, the Jew could at that point have been amply compensated in exchange for his cancellation of the contract. Having failed in the attempt at incorporation, Portia openly proceeds to use the power of Christian nationalism against him. Underlying the operational multiculturalism of that cosmopolitan Venetian law, which Shylock believed would facilitate the judicial murder of Antonio, is a legal structure designed to protect Christian Venice against aliens. It is within the harsh scope of this inequitable justice that Shylock has placed himself.

§

Jews and Christians, along with Muslims, represent what the Qur'an calls the "People of the Book". All are monotheists, worshipping one God; all claim spiritual descent from Abraham; all place a written scripture, understood as the Word of God, at the heart of the faith. And to a surprising extent, all three versions of this scripture have much in common. The Christian Bible subsumes the Jewish Scripture as the "Old Testament"; the Qur'an incorporates material from the Hebrew Bible and the New Testament.

These historical interactions produce a degree of theological commonality. In *The Merchant of Venice* Shylock quotes from the New Testament, and Antonio echoes the Old. Portia appeals to a common Judaeo-Christian intercession when she says: "We do pray for mercy,/And that same prayer doth teach us all to render/The deeds of mercy." When told he is to inherit Shylock's wealth, Lorenzo says:

> Fair ladies, you drop Manna in the way
> Of starved people.

(5.1.293)

The absent Shylock has mysteriously become YHWH feeding the children of Israel in the wilderness. If this is a Christian joke at the Jew's expense, it is a somewhat blasphemous one, as this story is hugely important in Christian theology: the exodus prefigures the redemption, and the bread of heaven the living bread of the Last Supper and the Eucharist. The story is mentioned in the Qur'an (Sura 20.80–81), and the idea of food delivered from heaven is at the centre of one of its chapters, "The Table".

The People of the Book cannot help speaking this common

language, even when they speak of enmity and hatred. In *The Merchant of Venice* Portia draws on the common resources of Judaism and Christianity to offer Shylock an ecumenical solution to the impasse of enmity, possible within the multicultural constitution of Venice. Shylock chooses hostility over friendship, money over freedom, law over justice. Here Shakespeare presents Christianity not in terms of its own doctrinal controversies, but rather in relation to its parent religion, Judaism, the Scriptures of which were of course incorporated into the Christian Bible. Shakespeare is in this play less interested in scrutinizing Christianity from the inside, and more interested in affirming its positive value in contradistinction to another world faith. He is less concerned with national religious culture, and more with the clashes and compromises possible between different religions on an international stage.

Chapter Eight

"A special providence": *HAMLET*

Conventionally thought of as not only Shakespeare's best work, but one of the greatest specimens of dramatic literature of all time, *Hamlet* is a deeply religious play, which throughout addresses crucial spiritual questions about life and death, good and evil, sin and repentance, authority and justice. It begins with a ghost emerging from the afterlife, and ends with a prayer for the soul of a dying prince. In the course of the drama Shakespeare's most loquacious hero discourses on such key religious questions as death, mourning, marriage, ritual, suicide, the afterlife, sin and repentance, the universe, providence, and justice. Even those who would prefer to discuss the play in terms of philosophy or ideology are compelled to acknowledge that it often articulates its ideas and convictions in a religious language. More recently *Hamlet* has become a particular focus of debates about the presence in Shakespeare's work of the Reformation, and of the Roman Catholic faith it suppressed and replaced.

§

Shakespeare's fictional Prince of Denmark, Hamlet (together with his friends Horatio, Rosencrantz, and Guildenstern), is declared in the play to have attended the real University of Wittenberg in Germany, which happened to be Martin Luther's university, and a seat of the Protestant Reformation. The university was founded in 1502, and Luther (as Shakespeare would surely have known) joined as Professor of Theology ("Doctor of Bible") in 1512. It was to the door of the *Schlosskirche*, the Castle Church of Wittenberg, that Luther is said to have nailed his "Ninety-five Theses" in 1517. No other place in the world could have associated Shakespeare's greatest play more strongly with the Reformation than Prince Hamlet's choice of college.

Here is Hamlet explaining to his university colleagues his state of mind:

> I have of late – but wherefore I know not – lost all my mirth, forgone all custom of exercises; and indeed it goes so heavily with my disposition that this goodly frame, the earth, seems to me a sterile promontory. This most excellent canopy the air, look you, this brave o'erhanging, this majestical roof fretted with golden fire, – why, it appears no other thing to me than a foul and pestilent congregation of vapours. What a piece of work is a man! how noble in reason, how infinite in faculty, in form and moving how express and admirable, in action how like an angel, in apprehension how like a god – the beauty of the world! The paragon of animals! And yet to me, what is this quintessence of dust? Man delights not me – no, nor woman neither…

(2.2.287–99)

Hamlet sees the world with a kind of double vision. On the one hand he can glimpse the paradisal beauty of the created world, "goodly", "excellent", "majestical", and the place within it of man as supreme creature, gifted with a godlike reason, infinitely capable, noble and beautiful, angelically rational, the very image of God's glory. On the other hand he sees the world as fallen, "sterile", contaminated and diseased, a "foul and pestilent congregation of vapours"; and humanity as nothing more than a "quintessence of dust". His imagination testifies to a perfect earth ruled by a rational humanity, while his disenchanted perception recognizes the world as fallen, and man as a contemptible creature without nobility or reason.

This passage has of course been interpreted as something more than an autobiographical description of Hamlet's mind, cast into melancholy and depression by the loss of his father, and his mother Gertrude's marriage to his despised uncle Claudius. Hamlet is speaking here as a philosopher, offering a critical view of the world and of humanity's place in it. His ideas have been compared to those of the great French Catholic philosopher Michel de Montaigne, who gave a modern accent to mediaeval pessimism and classical scepticism.

But the voice that reverberates through the speech of this Wittenberg-educated prince is surely that of the Protestant Reformation. Luther famously rejected the "similitude" theology that had developed from the early church fathers through Augustine and Aquinas, in which man retains certain capacities bestowed on him before the fall, in particular that of reason, and is capable of developing into the *imago dei*, the image of God. Where Catholic thinkers had argued that salvation is attainable by developing the higher powers of humanity towards a likeness of God, Luther insisted that faith alone was sufficient. In Luther's soteriology Christ came to human beings where they are, and as they are, and all the resources of salvation lie outside humanity: we cannot evolve towards God, or save ourselves by our own resources. For Luther the divine image has disappeared from man just as the original paradise had vanished. "The world was most beautiful from the beginning," he admitted, and humans were "righteous from the beginning". But now "from the image of God, from the knowledge of God, from the knowledge of all the other creatures, and from a very honourable nakedness man has fallen into blasphemies, into hatred, into contempt of God…" ("Lectures on Genesis", 1535).

§

If Hamlet is a Protestant prince, however, he is the son of a Catholic king, whose spirit declares that he has come directly from purgatory:

> I am thy father's spirit,
> Doomed for a certain term to walk the night,
> And for the day confined to fast in fires
> Till the foul crimes done in my days of nature
> Are burnt and purged away.

(1.5.9–13)

In "Doomed for a certain term", term was the length of time a soul has to spend in purgatory, according to mediaeval Catholic belief, enduring pain and punishment in order to be fitted for heaven. Souls were imagined as tormented by fire and other tortures – as painful in kind as the punishments of hell – but on a temporary basis, serving a sentence that would ultimately end in blissful release.

A late developing doctrine of the mediaeval Catholic Church, formulated in the twelfth century, purgatory became a central article of belief, and large parts of pre-Reformation church and social life were built around it. Between heaven and hell there was a middle place, where the souls of the dead could continue, through deserved punishment, to grow in love and understanding of God. Some went straight to heaven, some to hell: the absolutely saintly and the wholly damned. Most people, it was thought, would need some refinement before they could be regarded as sufficiently purified to enter the heavenly kingdom.

So in the Middle Ages the dead were thought of as existing in an intermediate place, enduring temporary punishment, and needing the assistance of the living. The church offered its services as an intercessor which could effect reductions in punishment via prayer, at a price. Here began the corrupt system of indulgences via which massive sums of money found their way into clergy hands through donations or bequests from people who hoped to shorten their own, or their loved ones', terms in purgatory.

According to the Church of England in 1600, when *Hamlet* appeared, there was no such thing as purgatory. Beginning with Henry VIII's dissolution of the monasteries, the whole apparatus established to pray for the dead was destroyed. Article XXII of the Articles of Religion (1563) dealt with purgatory:

> *The Romish Doctrine concerning Purgatory, Pardons, Worshipping, and Adoration, as well of Images as of Reliques, and also invocation of Saints, is a fond thing, vainly invented, and grounded upon no warranty of Scripture, but rather repugnant to the Word of God.*

That was early in Elizabeth's reign. Much later, at the time of *Hamlet*, King James I took the trouble to reinforce this article in his "Premonition" of 1609:

> *As for Purgatory, and all the trash depending thereupon, it is not worth the talking of; Bellarmine cannot find any ground for it in all the Scriptures. Only I would pray him to tell me, If that fair green meadow that is in Purgatory have a brook running through it, that in case I come there I may have hawking upon it. But as for me, I am sure there is a Heaven and a Hell, praenium et poena, for the Elect and Reprobate; how many other rooms there be, I am not on God His council. Multae sunt mansiones in domo Patris mei, ["there are many mansions in my father's house"] saith Christ, Who is the true*

> *purgatory for our sins. But how many chambers and ante-chambers*
> *the Devil hath, they can best tell that go to him. But in case there*
> *were more places for souls to go to than we know of, yet let us content*
> *us with that which in His Word He hath revealed unto us, and not*
> *inquire further into His secrets. Heaven and Hell are there revealed*
> *to be the eternal home of all mankind. Let us endeavour to win the*
> *one and eschew the other; and there is an end.*

Notwithstanding Shakespeare's own contemporary Protestant orthodoxy, Hamlet's father is decidedly Roman Catholic. Not only has he been murdered by a brother who then appropriated his widow, as a victim of assassination he has died without benefit of the sacraments:

> Cut off even in the blossoms of my sin,
> Unhouseled, dis-appointed, unaneled,
> No reck'ning made, but sent to my account
> With all my imperfections on my head.
> O, horrible, O, horrible, most horrible!

(1.5.76–80)

By using the word "unaneled", King Hamlet complains that he went to his death without the oil of extreme unction; and "unhouseled" means that he was denied the Eucharistic sacrament as part of the last rites. The pain arising from this deprivation of the sacrament is very much a Catholic anguish, since of course Protestantism denied that extreme unction was a sacrament at all.

As critics have pointed out, these sentiments were for Shakespeare very close to home. His own father's Catholic "Spiritual Testament", mentioned earlier, provides for a possible term in purgatory, and asks for Masses to be held, and prayers to be said, in order to deliver him from torment and pain:

I, John Shakspear, do in like manner pray and beseech all my dear friends, parents, and kinsfolks, by the bowels of our Saviour Jesus Christ, that since it is uncertain what lot will befall me, for fear notwithstanding lest by reason of my sins I be to pass and stay a long while in Purgatory, they will vouchsafe to assist and succour me with their holy prayers and satisfactory works, especially with the holy sacrifice of the mass, as being the most effectual means to deliver souls from their torments and pains; from the which, If I shall by God's gracious goodness and by their virtuous works be delivered, I do promise that I will not be ungrateful unto them, for so great a benefit.

As we saw in Chapter 2, the same document expresses the hope that John will, at his death, receive the sacrament of extreme unction.

I, John Shakspear, do protest that I will also pass out of this life, armed with the last sacrament of extreme unction: the which if through any let or hindrance I should not then be able to have, I do now also for that time demand and crave the same…

Shakespeare's father did not die until 1601, by which time *Hamlet* was already in the theatre, though it was not published until 1603. But his son Hamnet had died at the age of eleven in 1596. Biographers and critics have focused on family bereavement as one of the key emotional drivers of *Hamlet*, suggesting that the ghost who returns from a Catholic past demanding traditional pre-Reformation rites and prayers was a compound of Shakespeare's dead son, buried by the rites of the Church of England, and his soon-to-be-dead father, whose Catholic religious demands had been clearly set out in the document quoted above.

§

The ghost in *Hamlet* does not however ask for Masses and prayers, but for something quite different: revenge.

> If thou didst ever thy dear father love…
> Revenge his foul and most unnatural murder.

(1.5.23, 25)

Despite the context of Catholic language and ritual invoking purgatory, prayer for the dead and the seven sacraments, when the ghost bids Hamlet "remember" him, it is not for purposes of intercession, but to provoke the son to the non-Christian obligation of avenging his murdered father:

> Remember thee?
> Ay, thou poor ghost, while memory holds a seat
> In this distracted globe. Remember thee?
> Yea, from the table of my memory
> I'll wipe away all trivial fond records,
> All saws of books, all forms, all pressures past,
> That youth and observation copied there,
> And thy commandment all alone shall live
> Within the book and volume of my brain
> Unmixed with baser matter…

(1.5.95–104)

Here Hamlet makes the extraordinary promise to expunge the entire contents of his education and replace it with a single "commandment" – revenge. Despite the pervasive echoes of the Eucharist, a ritual designed both to "remember" Christ's redeeming sacrifice on the cross, and to endorse the "commandments" given at the Last Supper ("A new commandment give I unto you, that ye love one another: as I have loved you, that ye also love one another" – John 13:34), this vow of commemoration has little to do with Christianity, harking back as it does to the revenge code of the pagan Scandinavian society from which the story of Hamlet derives. Hamlet senior was in Shakespeare's characterization clearly capable of reconciling the incompatible demands of Catholic piety, including sensitivities about appropriate use of the sacraments, with the revenge ethics of the Scandinavian warrior culture. In Shakespeare's time both state and church preached vehemently against private revenge, often citing (as does the Elizabethan homily "Against Contention and Brawling", regularly read in churches) Romans 12:19: "Dearly beloved, avenge not yourselves, but give place unto wrath: for it is written, Vengeance is mine: I will repay, saith the Lord." Hamlet's vow of revenge sets him into conflict with his own Renaissance Christian culture, and with the Reformation education he is assumed to have experienced at Wittenberg. And this clash of cultures is arguably the key dramatic conflict that drives the play.

Following the death of Polonius, Hamlet comes upon Claudius at prayer. Before he enters, Claudius reveals to the audience the tormented condition of his conscience. He is confessing, not to a priest, but directly to God:

> O, my offence is rank! It smells to heaven.
> It hath the primal eldest curse upon't,
> A brother's murder…

(3.3.36–38)

We have already observed several uses by Shakespeare of the biblical Cain and Abel story. Here Claudius is Cain; he has assassinated his innocent brother and thus inherited Cain's primordial guilt – "the primal eldest curse", the guilt of the very first murder. Claudius draws on the play's abundant imagery of decay and corruption (for example, "something is rotten in the state of Denmark"), suggesting that the spiritual stench of his guilt can reach as far as heaven. Claudius is desperate to pray, but he finds himself incapable:

> Pray can I not.
> Though inclination be as sharp as will,
> My stronger guilt defeats my strong intent,
> And like a man to double business bound,
> I stand in pause where I shall first begin,
> And both neglect.

(3.3.38–43)

Claudius describes himself in what we now call a "catch-22" situation, called to do two incompatible things at once, "like a man to double business bound". He longs to open his heart to God in repentance, but his guilt defeats his object. He knows that grace is there waiting for him, the gates of mercy are never closed, and God can absolve him of his sins:

> What if this cursed hand
> Were thicker than itself with brother's blood,
> Is there not rain enough in the sweet heavens
> To wash it white as snow?

(3.3.41–44)

The image of rain washing his bloodstained hand "white as snow" alludes of course to the language of baptism, traditionally practised on Whit (White) Sunday (Henry V speaks of the conscience "washed/As pure as sin with baptism"). So what prevents Claudius from repenting? He is prepared to confess his guilt and pray for forgiveness: "Forgive me my foul murder". But to follow through on this confession would require a genuine amendment of life, the renunciation of everything he has gained from his crime:

> That cannot be, since I am still possessed
> Of those effects for which I did the murder –
> My crown, mine own ambition and my queen.
> May one be pardoned and retain th'offence?

(3.3.53–56)

As *The Book of Common Prayer* exhorts, "bewail your own sinful lives… confess yourselves to almighty God, with full purpose of amendment of life". Claudius finds himself in an insoluble self-division, split between pious words and sinful thoughts: "My words fly up, my thoughts remain below:/Words without thoughts never to heaven go" (3.4.97–98). It is at this maximal point of Claudius's spiritual struggle that Hamlet comes upon him, and his first thought is of his revenge. The king is alone, defenceless and easily killed.

> *Ham.* Now might I do it pat, now he is praying,
> And now I'll do't, and so he goes to heaven,
> And so am I revenged.

(3.3.73–78)

We imagine, or witness, Hamlet drawing his sword and preparing to assassinate the kneeling king. But he hesitates, and considers how his action would be subsequently interpreted:

> That would be scanned,
> A villain kills my father; and for that
> I, his sole son, do this same villain send
> To heaven.

(3.3.75–78)

Because Claudius is at prayer, possibly absolved from his sins and ready for death, Hamlet assumes his soul will go straight to heaven. This is not what he intends at all.

> O, this is hire and salary, not revenge!
> A took my father grossly, full of bread,
> With all his crimes broad blown, as flush as May;
> And how his audit stands, who knows save heaven?
> But in our circumstance and course of thought
> 'Tis heavy with him. And am I then revenged
> To take him in the purging of his soul,
> When he is fit and season'd for his passage?

(3.3.79–86)

Here the Protestant prince attributes a striking importance to the sacraments. His father died without preparation, without extreme unction, without absolution, and as his son knows, is suffering in purgatory. To kill Claudius with his soul already "purged", ensuring he would go straight to heaven, would be an act of mercy unthinkable to a revenger. And so Hamlet resolves to defer, to delay, to kill him on another occasion, and thereby consign his soul directly to hell.

> Up, sword, and know thou a more horrid hint.
> When he is drunk asleep, or in his rage,
> Or in th'incestuous pleasure of his bed,
> At gaming, swearing, or about some act
> That has no relish of salvation in't;
> Then trip him that his heels may kick at heaven,
> And that his soul may be as damned and black
> As hell whereto it goes.

(3.3.88–95)

What Hamlet is doing here is assuming the theatrical role of revenger, playing it for all it is worth, without actually implementing the deed the revenger is there to perform. The prince's famous "delay" or "procrastination" is never explicitly defined as a religious scruple about the justice of revenge. But something holds Hamlet back, despite his promise to the ghost, despite his resolve to efface all his knowledge and understanding in favour of the one vindictive "commandment". He will do almost anything, it sometimes seems, to avoid committing to the act of revenge, including extensive soliloquizing and conversation, instructing actors in dramatic craft, producing a play, killing somebody else (though possibly in mistake for the king), and in particular forcing his mother into a rigorous examination of her own conscience.

§

The ghost had expressly instructed his son to leave Gertrude alone:

> Taint not thy mind, nor let thy soul contrive
> Against thy mother aught. Leave her to heaven,
> And to those thorns that in her bosom lodge
> To prick and sting her.

(1.5.85–88)

The ghost does not want Gertrude publicly exposed and shamed. But Hamlet deliberately goes to his mother's chamber in order to subject her to an aggressive spiritual examination, in which he openly accuses her of complicity in her husband's murder:

> A bloody deed – almost as bad, good-mother,
> As kill a king and marry with his brother.

(3.4.27–28)

Hamlet's purpose in placing Gertrude under such an inquisition is to motivate her own self-knowledge and provoke her to remorse over her sins. To do this he shows her pictures of Claudius and Hamlet senior: one resembles a god, the other a stalk of rotten corn, a "mildewed ear". The only force that could attract her from one to the other is lust, of which Gertrude should be heartily ashamed:

> O shame, where is thy blush? Rebellious hell,
> If thou canst mutine in a matron's bones,
> To flaming youth let virtue be as wax
> And melt in her own fire.

(3.4.72–75)

Initially resistant, Gertrude is compelled by Hamlet's insistent exhortations to look into her own heart, and to confess that she is guilty, though without naming her crime:

> O Hamlet, speak no more!
> Thou turn'st mine eyes into my very soul,
> And there I see such black and grained spots
> As will not leave their tinct...
> O, speak to me no more!
> These words like daggers enter in mine ears.
> No more, sweet Hamlet!

(3.4.78–86)

Hamlet is not behaving like a Catholic priest, asking Gertrude to enumerate her sins and confess them in order to obtain absolution. Still less does he point her in the direction of a church or a confessional. The objective of his exhortation is rather the Protestant one of forcing his mother to examine herself, to perform an inward audit of the sins she has committed, and to lay them before God in private prayer. Hamlet's methodology is closer to that of the English Puritans, who were encouraged to examine their actions and conscience daily for signs of God's dispensation, and to note down what they discovered in a journal (we know that Hamlet kept a journal from his reference to "my tables"), than it is to the Roman Catholic sacrament of penance. Reformed Christians confessed, not to a priest, but to paper, to themselves, and thence directly to God. We do not have to seek far to find evidence of this penitential system in Shakespeare's everyday world. Here is the Exhortation preceding Holy Communion in the 1559 *Book of Common Prayer*:

> *My duty is to exhort you to consider the dignity of the holy mystery, and the great peril of the unworthy receiving thereof, and so to search and examine your own consciences, as you should come holy and clean to a most godly and heavenly feast… First, to examine your lives and conversation by the rule of God's commandments and wherinsoever ye shall perceive your selves to have offended, either by will, word, or deed, there bewail your own sinful lives, confess your selves to almighty God, with full purpose of amendment of life.*

The 1559 service even follows Luther in allowing the possibility of informal confession to a priest:

> *… if there be any of you, which by the means aforesaid cannot quiet his own conscience, but requireth further comfort or counsel, then let him come to me, or some other discrete and learned minister of God's word, and open his grief, that he may receive such ghostly counsel, advise, and comfort, as his conscience may be relieved, and*

that by the ministry of God's word, he may receive comfort, and the benefit of absolution, to the quieting of his conscience, and avoiding of all scruple and doubtfulness.

But Luther did not acknowledge penance as a sacrament, and neither does *The Book of Common Prayer*, which Hamlet follows precisely as he closes his examination of Gertrude:

> *Ham.* Confess yourself to heaven;
> Repent what's past, avoid what is to come…

(3.4.140–41)

Forgive us all that is past;
and grant that we may ever hereafter
serve and please thee, in newness of life,
to the honour and glory of thy name…

(*Book of Common Prayer*)

§

Right up to this final point Hamlet wants to see himself as a free agent, exercising free will, but recognizes that in fact he is trapped inside a predetermined course of events: "I could be bounded in a nutshell, and count myself as king of infinite space." You can hope to be anything you want, but you cannot reason your way out of a nutshell. As Calvin puts it, our free will is actually God's plan:

By his providence, not heaven and earth and inanimate creatures only, but also the counsels and wills of men are so governed as to move exactly in the course which he has destined.

(*Institutes of the Christian Religion*, 1.16.8)

For most of the first four acts of the play Hamlet struggles against his election, trying to escape from the constraints of this "nutshell" life, which has only one possible course, one final destination. With the accidental killing of Polonius we see him beginning to take action, though it is by no means clear how the actions he takes might contribute to the actualization of his predestined election. This is only to be expected, however, since as Calvin argues, providence is inscrutable:

> *I say then, that though all things are ordered by the counsel and certain arrangement of God, to us, however, they are fortuitous – not because we imagine that Fortune rules the world and mankind, and turns all things upside down at random (far be such a heartless thought from every Christian breast); but as the order, method, end, and necessity of events, are, for the most part, hidden in the counsel of God, though it is certain that they are produced by the will of God...*

(*Institutes*, 1.16.9)

During Hamlet's absence from Denmark he not only becomes the man of action his destiny requires – as is made clear in his narrative of his daring escape from the ship and his adventure with the pirates – but also comes to realize that his freedom is God's necessity.

> Not a whit. We defy augury. There's a special providence in the fall of a sparrow. If it be now, 'tis not to come. If it be not to come, it will be now. If it be not now, yet it will come. The readiness is all. Since no man has aught of what he leaves, what is't to leave betimes?

(5.2.157–61)

Here Hamlet alludes to Matthew:

> *Are not two sparrows sold for a farthing, and one of them shall not*
> *fall on the ground without your Father?*
> *Yea, and all the hairs of your head are numbered.*
> *Fear ye not therefore, ye are of more value than many sparrows.*

(Matthew 10:29–31)

"Special providence" was of course Calvin's own term for defining the operation of the universe:

> *God is a Governor and Preserver, and that, not by producing a kind*
> *of general motion in the machine of the globe as well as in each*
> *of its parts, but by a special Providence sustaining, cherishing,*
> *superintending, all the things which he has made, to the very*
> *minutest, even to a sparrow.*

(*Institutes*, 1.16.1)

And Christ's words from Matthew on the fall of the sparrow formed one of Calvin's favourite examples of God's providential government.

> *Hence, our Saviour, after declaring that even a sparrow falls*
> *not to the ground without the will of his Father (Matt 10:29),*
> *immediately makes the application, that being more valuable than*
> *many sparrows, we ought to consider that God provides more*
> *carefully for us (Matt 10:31).*

(*Institutes*, 1.16.5)

Once he is reconciled to Calvinist theology, Hamlet has no further doubts or scruples about his destiny. He feels that now everything is in the open – Claudius is manifestly his father's murderer and a usurper, and has made an attempt on Hamlet's own life – he can at last reconcile his obligation of revenge with a conception of true justice.

> Does it not, think'st thee, stand me now upon –
> He that hath killed my king and whored my mother,
> Popped in between th'election and my hopes,
> Thrown out his angle for my proper life,
> And with such coz'nage – is't not perfect conscience
> To quit him with this arm? And is't not to be damn'd,
> To let this canker of our nature come
> In further evil?

(5.2.64–71)

In the final scene Hamlet plays along with the staged duel, fully aware of the dangers to himself (he has after all murdered Laertes' father, thus becoming the target of the same revenge ethic to which he is bound, and he knows Claudius wants him dead). But the narrative evolves to a predetermined end. Hamlet kills Claudius, but not before Laertes has confessed to the plot; Hamlet himself is already fatally poisoned by Laertes' sword, and Gertrude is dead from the poisoned cup intended for him. In this context of declared, confessed, and revealed guilt, engineered in partnership by the dramatist and by the will of God, to kill Claudius is an act of execution.

All that remains for Hamlet is to ensure that his story is fully and truly told, a task he assigns to his loyal friend Horatio:

> O God, Horatio, what a wounded name,
> Things standing thus unknown, shall live behind me!
> If thou didst ever hold me in thy heart
> Absent thee from felicity awhile,
> And in this harsh world draw thy breath in pain
> To tell my story… Horatio, I am dead,

> Thou liv'st. Report me and my cause aright
> To the unsatisfied.

(5.2.286–91; 280–82)

To the very end Hamlet is anxious that his "cause" should be understood not as a random and arbitrary career of "casual slaughter", but as a narrative with a shape, a form, a meaning: as the working out of a "special providence". And so he dies; and, in Horatio's mind at least, goes not to any intermediate realm of purgatory, but straight to a Protestant heaven:

> Now cracks a noble heart. Good night sweet prince:
> And flights of angels sing thee to thy rest!

(5.2.302–303)

CHAPTER NINE

"INCOMPREHENSIBLE JUSTICE":
KING LEAR

In the preceding chapter I referred to *Hamlet* as "Shakespeare's best work", a status it certainly enjoyed through the nineteenth century and most of the twentieth. But following the Second World War *Hamlet* was replaced, in the view of many critics, by *King Lear* as Shakespeare's greatest tragedy. *King Lear* has been widely considered a play that can be read and performed as a revelation of, and a commentary on, what is often thought of as one of the bleakest periods in human history. Its portrayal of a society descending into anarchy and chaos, as its protagonists reveal the most savage and cruel capabilities of inhumanity, seems to resonate particularly with our world of unceasing civil conflicts, violence and cruelty, torture and genocide; a world of arbitrary arrest and secret executions in prison, of internment and death camps, of treachery and betrayal; a world in which "Humanity must perforce prey on itself, like monsters of the deep" (4.2.49–50).

§

When I first studied *King Lear* in the 1950s, critical opinion held the play to be a parable of Christian sacrifice and spiritual regeneration. The most influential interpretation was that of G. Wilson Knight in *The Wheel of Fire*, who saw the play as a Christian narrative of "creative suffering". Men and women are ennobled by suffering, which confers on them a deeper understanding both of human nature and of the secret purposes of existence, enriches them, and gives them peace. From about 1960 onwards these redemptive interpretations of *King Lear* were replaced by nihilistic readings, and *Lear* became a drama depicting the ethical vacuity and moral exhaustion of the modern world. The textbook example of this reading was Jan Kott's *Shakespeare Our Contemporary*. Kott equated the landscape of *King Lear* with the bleak modernism of Samuel Beckett. He called his essay "King Lear or Endgame", suggesting a parallel with Beckett's empty, godless universe, and read the play as atheist and nihilist. Lear, in this reading, strips away all pretence in order to show the nothingness of human existence, like the peeling of an onion. For Kott the play tragically mocks all religious claims: there is no heaven on earth, and no heaven beyond.

Both views can easily be located in the play:

> *Gloucester.* As flies to wanton boys are we to th'gods;
> They kill us for their sport.

(4.1.37–38)

> *Lear.* Upon such sacrifices, my Cordelia,
> The gods themselves throw incense.

(5.3.20–21)

Is *King Lear* an uplifting affirmation of the possibilities of spiritual redemption, or a bleak invocation of a universe ruled by indifferent or malicious powers? Do the "gods" of the play throw incense on sacrifice, or callously and wantonly kill men and women like flies? These alternatives remain in place as options for reading *King Lear*. If we interpret the play as a morality tale in which suffering brings redemption, we are reading it within a Christian framework. If we understand the play as a portrait of human savagery played out against the backdrop of an indifferent or malicious universe, we are locating it within a non-Christian paradigm. The line alluding to the dead or dying Cordelia – "Look on her lips, look there" – to one school of interpretation is evidence of redemption, even of immortality; to another an even more cruel twist of tragedy's wounding knife. Some call it a "cruel final delusion"; some a "blessed liberation".

A problem for any religious reading of *King Lear* is that the play is set in a pre-Christian Britain. The story derived from legendary histories which placed Lear's reign in the early fourth century, when Britain was under Roman occupation, shortly before Christianity began to be established under Constantine. Shakespeare's play imagines Britain as a national kingdom prior to the arrival of the Romans. Lear's kingdom has no church, no bishops, no clergy, and any religious language used by the characters refers vaguely to "the gods", or names specific classical deities, such as Apollo, who were of course worshipped in Roman Britain. This has rendered the play easier to interpret as an agnostic or even atheist work, which provides no evidence of any benevolent higher power at work in the world, since the Greek and Roman gods could not be taken seriously as divine beings, and depicts human life as cruel and savage, brutish and short. On the other hand the world of *King Lear* is not a carefully documented and historically sourced depiction of a past society, comparable to Shakespeare's Roman plays, in which the characters adopt and display the belief systems proper to their time. The people of Lear's kingdom swear by classical deities, fear the dark powers of sorcery and witchcraft and alternately promote or dismiss astrology. But running through the play is an undercurrent of Christian belief, which shows itself in specifically Christian language, doctrine, and theology.

§

What kind of play was *King Lear* when it was first written and produced in the theatre? The first printed edition carried the following title: *M. William Shak-speare: his true chronicle historie of the life and death of King Lear and his three daughters.*

When the play was printed (in a somewhat different version) as part of Shakespeare's collected works in 1623, the "First Folio", it was under the simplified title *The Tragedie of King Lear*. Here the name contains the text within a distinct genre – tragedy.

The play is certainly a tragedy. The old king, Lear, unwisely renounces his power and banishes his youngest daughter Cordelia, who is treated shamefully by her older sisters, and he eventually goes mad. In the sub-plot another father, Gloucester, rejects his loyal child, and lives to regret the error; captured by Lear's daughters, he is tortured and blinded. Later Lear is reconciled with Cordelia, but then they are both captured and Cordelia is killed. The play ends with Lear carrying on the corpse of his murdered daughter, and then dying himself. All the bad characters die, but most of the good ones too. Tragedy strikes the innocent and the guilty alike.

So is the play a tragedy or a history? The Quarto title, *his true chronicle historie of the life and death of King Lear and his three daughters*, suggests a legendary kind of history close to fairy tale. The King Lear story derived ultimately from a twelfth-century chronicle, *Historia Regum Britanniae* (c. 1136) by Geoffrey of Monmouth, which tells of the kings who ruled in Britain in pre-Christian times. Geoffrey claimed to have based his history on books in the language of the ancient Britons, that is, modern-day Welsh. Academics have regarded Geoffrey's work as more legend than history, so the two overlap in Shakespeare's primary source. Certainly "King Lear and his three daughters" sounds more like a fairy tale than a work of history.

This uncertainty of genre is one of the reasons why this play has such a varied reputation, and why it has been so widely interpreted in criticism and on stage and screen. During the course of its four centuries of existence, *King Lear* has been notoriously unstable both as a text and in its performance in the theatre. If you could go back and see any production of *King Lear* in any theatre between 1681 and 1823, you would find the plot quite different from the familiar Shakespearean action. You would find the language entirely rewritten, into heroic couplets. For that space of 142 years, when Cordelia says she does not want to marry the king of France, there is a good reason for it. She already has a lover: Gloucester's son Edgar. There was no trace of the Fool in the play, a character who must have been a favourite in the seventeenth century, and who became a central figure for modern criticism. Above all, the play was no longer a tragedy. Within seventy-three years of its original publication in 1608, it had acquired a happy ending. Cordelia and Edgar manage between them to defeat the powers of the older daughters, and to restore Lear to his throne.

Neither Lear nor Cordelia dies in this version. Cordelia is instead rescued, first from rape and then from hanging, by her lover Edgar. The play ends with Edgar renouncing any claim he might have as victor over the kingdom, preferring to join Cordelia in a romantic retirement. We know the closing lines of the play from Shakespeare – Edgar's:

> The weight of this sad time we must obey;
> Speak what we feel, not what we ought to say.
> The oldest hath borne most; we that are young
> Shall never see so much, nor live so long.

(5.3.322–25)

The victors seem to feel defeated; silenced; inheriting a world in which life has already been used up by the previous generation. But for a century and a half they appeared in a radically altered form, though still spoken by Edgar:

> Our drooping country now erects her head,
> Peace spreads her balmy wings, and plenty blooms.
> Divine Cordelia, all the gods can witness
> How much thy love to Empire I prefer!
> Thy bright example shall convince the world
> (Whatever storms of Fortune are decreed)
> That truth and [virtue] shall at last succeed.

(Nahum Tate, *The History of King Lear*, 1681)

"Succeed" hints there at a double meaning, with the primary sense "emerge with success" further suggesting "inherit power by succession". This play could be described as a political romance, concluding with a "happy ending", entailing the restoration of a previously abdicated monarchy.

Nahum Tate, author of this adaptation, was writing after exactly such a "Restoration" in 1660 – the Restoration of the Stuart monarchy after the English Civil War. He was also deploying the standard contemporary practice of regarding Shakespeare's plays as texts to be adapted and rewritten, virtually translated into what was considered the more polished and civilized language of the day. But even in such a context Tate's alteration of *King Lear* from tragedy to comedy, and the strikingly long period of currency and popularity enjoyed by that adaptation, still seem remarkable.

The most obvious change introduced is that of the happy ending, which helps to convert the dramatic action from tragedy to romance: from a narrative in which innocence and weakness are mercilessly punished along with the guilty, to one in which virtue and proper sentiment are rewarded with romantic reconciliation and the restoration of legitimacy. In its day Tate's adaptation was popular and highly esteemed. Dr Johnson preferred it to Shakespeare's.

In modern criticism it has been ridiculed as a travesty of Shakespeare by critics who assume the Shakespearean drama as the "original" of which Tate's adaptation was a corruption, the norm from which Tate manifestly deviated. Not surprisingly they see it as a wrong turn in the afterlife of the play. This is not, however, the only way of looking at it. Shakespeare did not invent the "King Lear" story. It was a traditional historical legend with a long ancestry, existing in a large number of different retellings, some of them in Shakespeare's time relatively recent. The versions of the story most likely to have influenced Shakespeare's version are (i) the reign of Lear recounted as part of the history of early Britain in Holinshed's *Chronicles*; (ii) the story as narrated in Book 2 of Spenser's *The Faerie Queene*; and (iii) an anonymous play entitled *The True Chronicle Historie of King Leir*, performed in the 1590s and published in 1605. The most striking feature of these different legendary and historical narratives, from the perspective of a comparison between Shakespeare and Tate, is that all these versions tell the same story as Tate's adaptation. The "King Lear" story is a historical romance narrative of restoration, with a happy ending, in all versions but those exemplified by Shakespeare's play.

In these legendary histories Lear's restoration is followed later by a tragic sequel. Lear is succeeded by Cordelia, who reigns as "supreme governesse of Britaine". After her husband's death, her nephews (the sons of Gonorill and Ragen), "disdaining to be under the government of a woman", rebel and imprison her. Cordelia was "laid… fast in ward, wherewith she tooke such grief, being a woman of manlie courage, and despairing to recouer libertie, there she slue hirselfe". What Shakespeare did was to telescope these two narratives, the romance and the history, into one tragic story. The tragic sequel to the traditional chronicle history was thus incorporated into the Shakespearean version, though as assassination rather than suicide.

The three most significant generic contexts influencing the Lear plays are history, romance, and tragedy. As exemplified in Holinshed, the Lear tale is a historical narrative of legitimacy, power, political authority, and military struggle: a story of a kingdom divided, invaded, and reunited. But the history is a very remote one, going back to a time about which little was known – Britain before the Romans. So the history is legendary and mythical, strongly coloured by romance. This is apparent in the versions of Spenser and the anonymous source play *The True Chronicle Historie of King Leir*. Within the framework of a historical and political narrative the Lear story generates folk tale and romance motifs of banishment and exile, recognition and return, disguise and mistaken identity.

§

These different conventions are all working together in the great opening scene, where King Lear sets out formally to divide his kingdom between his three daughters and their prospective husbands. This is history as seventeenth-century people understood it: a king, a court, dukes and earls, and foreign monarchs. The characters speak as if they are making history. The king's voice is the voice of power:

> Know that we have divided
> In three our kingdom; and 'tis our fast intent
> To shake all cares and business from our age,
> Conferring them on younger strengths, while we
> Unburthened crawl toward death. Our son of Cornwall,
> And you, our no less loving son of Albany,

> We have this hour a constant will to publish
> Our daughters' several dowers, that future strife
> May be prevented now. The princes, France and
> Burgundy,
> Great rivals in our youngest daughter's love,
> Long in our court have made their amorous sojourn,
> And here are to be answer'd.

(1.1.35–46)

This is a momentous event, like a coronation or the death of a king. What is said here cannot easily be taken back or amended. In one sense the occasion resembles the formal ceremony in which subjects swear fealty to a king. But underlying the historical narrative there lies an older archetype, a folk tale in which a father imposes a "love-test" on his three daughters. Two of them respond appropriately with elaborate speeches of insincere devotion. Cordelia, the only one who truly loves him, declines to do this, and replies with an act of civil disobedience: "Nothing, my lord."

"Let it be so," says Lear, displeased with the favourite daughter who will not answer him with the words of love he demands:

> For, by the sacred radiance of the sun,
> The mysteries of Hecate, and the night;
> By all the operation of the orbs
> From whom we do exist, and cease to be;
> Here I disclaim all my paternal care,
> Propinquity and property of blood,
> And as a stranger to my heart and me
> Hold thee from this, for ever. The barbarous Scythian,
> Or he that makes his generation messes
> To gorge his appetite, shall to my bosom

Be as well neighboured, pitied, and relieved,
As thou my sometime daughter.

(1.1.109–19)

Lear's religious frame of reference here is pagan, as he invokes the secret rites of Hecate, ancient Greek goddess of darkness, and astrology, the influence of the stars on the human condition. He compares Cordelia to the Scythians, a Middle Eastern people associated by the Greeks and Romans with cannibalism, patricide, and (interestingly) inarticulacy. The term "barbarous" derives from a Greek word that means both "foreign" and "stammering" or "jabbering" – a foreigner is one whose language cannot be understood, as Lear fails to understand Cordelia's.

This classical background and complex etymology underpins Lear's language, which is highly formal and ceremonial. It is complex, Latinate, full of ornate words, like the swearing of a formal oath on a ceremonial occasion, a wedding or a coronation. But what's *happening* here is typical of romance. This is a fundamental romance archetype: the favourite royal child abandoned by her father because of a misunderstanding. It resembles stories in which there are three choices, or three questions, or three chances to get something right. This is the realm of fairy tale, though Shakespeare adds some details of Christian language to the romance, as when the king of France accepts Cordelia without the promised dowry –

Fairest Cordelia, that art most rich, being poor;
Most choice, forsaken; and most loved, despised!

(1.1.251–52)

– which directly alludes to 2 Corinthians 6:10: "as poor, and *yet* making many rich: as having nothing, and *yet* possessing all things". Already the play is beginning to polarize wealth and poverty, weakness and power, sophistication and simplicity, plainness and ceremony in dualisms that recall the crucial controversies of the Reformation.

Other romance elements include the story of Kent, a loyal courtier banished for honest speaking, who re-enters his master's service in disguise, and the Gloucester sub-plot, with the good brother disinherited by deception, disguised as a beggar until the time is ripe for him to reveal himself. At the end of the play Edgar returns as the anonymous challenger of the mediaeval chivalric romances, emerging from nowhere to defeat the villain in single combat and claim the kingdom. Again the play is investing in romance, legend, fairy tale.

On the other hand Shakespeare's play is undoubtedly a tragedy. Lear's abdication of power releases an anarchy of competing appetites and interests that splits the kingdom asunder. No sooner have the other two daughters, Goneril and Regan, been given their share of the kingdom than they are seen plotting to get rid of the old king. That scene is followed with one in which Gloucester's illegitimate son Edmund proclaims the rights of "bastards", and plots to expropriate his brother Edgar's inheritance. This he embarks on by forging an incriminating letter from Edgar and showing it to his father, which prompts Gloucester to disown his loyal son, just as Lear has discarded his loving daughter. Edmund's philosophy, expressed in powerful soliloquies, is a belief in the absolute freedom of the human will, unfettered by astrological influence or worldly morality. Men and women are made what they are by their own choices, decisions and actions. Edmund's thinking has been compared to that of Machiavelli, or the later liberal philosophy of Thomas Hobbes. This kind of atheist existentialism makes Edmund a very modern figure. But the debate over free will was at the time of the play more a theological than a political issue, particularly within Calvinism. Edmund's libertarian beliefs run counter to the dominant belief system of the play, and he is very much the villain of the piece.

When Goneril and Regan join forces to oppose Lear and to challenge his authority, Lear very quickly begins to realize he was wrong about Cordelia. Robbed of all respect and dignity, and accompanied by only a small band of loyal followers, Lear finds himself exposed to the storm, loses his wits, and discovers the essence of humanity in poverty and homelessness:

> Poor naked wretches, whereso'er you are
> That bide the pelting of this pitiless storm,
> How shall your houseless heads and unfed sides,
> Your looped and windowed raggedness, defend you
> From seasons such as these? O, I have ta'en
> Too little care of this! Take physic, pomp;
> Expose thyself to feel what wretches feel,
> That thou mayst shake the superflux to them,
> And show the heavens more just.

(3.4.29–37)

Lear's fellow feeling and compassion for the poor is not identified as specifically Christian, and can thus be persuasively read as expressing a humanist conception of worldly justice, calling for an irreversible shift of wealth and power from the wealthy to the dispossessed. But Lear's perspective is theological rather than political: the point of achieving justice on earth would be to demonstrate such justice as the effect of divine providence, to "show the heavens more just". In addition, scholars have suggested that the unusual word "superflux" is probably derived from a strident anti-Catholic polemic (extensively used by Shakespeare in *King Lear*), *A Declaration of Egregious Popish*

Impostures (1603) by Samuel Harsnett, a Cambridge scholar who later became Archbishop of York. The term is used in Harsnett's pamphlet in a passage savagely attacking Catholic priests as "imposturing renegadoes that come fresh from the Pope's tiring-house, masked with the vizard of holy burning zeal", who ostentatiously display their "lighter superfluities" until "God's revengeful arm doth uncase them to the view of the world, and then they suffer the mild stroke of justice". Thus Shakespeare has chosen to articulate Lear's vision of justice, which entails the removal of "pomp" and the redistribution of excessive wealth, the "superflux", in a Protestant language. Confronted with the disguised Edgar's naked body, Lear tries to remove his own clothes in an effort to strip down humanity to its essence: "thou art the thing itself; unaccommodated man is no more but such a poor, bare, forked animal as thou art" (3.4.98–100).

These tragic insights conduct the drama to a tragic end. The "evil" characters of the play – Goneril, Regan, the duke of Cornwall, Edmund – all meet with violent deaths. But the "good" characters also fall in the general melee. Gloucester dies peacefully, recognizing his true son Edgar, but Cordelia is brutally executed on Edmund's orders. The play ends with the death of Lear. But despite the overwhelming tragic catastrophe, *King Lear* remains pervaded by an ambiguity derived from its different narrative conventions and sources. There is always a tension between the dominant genre of tragedy and the ancient lines of the romance narrative. Inside the tragedy of *King Lear* is a happy ending trying to get out.

§

With Lear's insanity, the torturing of Gloucester, Edmund's success, the play rushes toward the supremacy of disaster. With Cordelia's return in Act 4, the arrival of allied troops, and the continuing determined passive resistance of Kent and Edgar, it turns away toward the once familiar happy ending of restorative romance. These implications are clear in a scene in which Kent and a gentleman describe Cordelia's return to Britain:

> *Kent.* Did your letters pierce the queen to any
> demonstration of grief?
> *Gent.* Ay, sir; she took them, in my presence;
> And now and then an ample tear trilled down
> Her delicate cheek. It seemed she was a queen
> Over her passion, who, most rebel-like,
> Sought to be king o'er her... There she shook
> The holy water from her heavenly eyes,
> And clamour moistened. Then away she started
> To deal with grief alone.
> *Kent.* It is the stars,
> The stars above us, govern our conditions;
> Else one self mate and make could not beget
> Such different issues.

(4.3.9–14; 28–34)

Here power has changed hands and is no longer, as in real political situations, in the grip of the great ones of history. Authority has passed to the fairy-tale "good daughter" who has come back, despite everything, to save her father. Cordelia is a queen of feeling and a figure of sanctity rather than a monarch of Britain, her tears declaring her sincerity and sacredness. She even seems to carry a religious aura, a kind of holiness, as she shakes "the holy water from her heavenly eyes". Kent wonders at the paradox of sibling difference, how one daughter can prove true and the two others false, a blend of fairy-tale poetic justice and Calvinist election. But at this point in the action, Cordelia seems to be the one who is destined to rule. Romance seems to be on the ascendant, poised to defeat tragedy. The exiled daughter has returned, and assumed the authority of queen. With her she brings forgiveness, reconciliation, pity for the oppressed, restoration of true authority. Here the discrepancy between the traditional happy ending and the bitter tragedy is stretched to a painful tension, as the dramatic action seems to be moving literally in two quite opposite directions.

This tension is at its greatest in Act 4, where Lear and Cordelia meet again for the first time since their separation. Cordelia brings with her a language of healing and restoration:

> *Cord.* O you kind gods,
> Cure this great breach in his abused nature!
> The untuned and jarring senses, O, wind up
> Of this child-changed father!…
> How does my royal lord? How fares your majesty?
> *Lear.* You do me wrong to take me out o' the grave.
> Thou art a soul in bliss; but I am bound
> Upon a wheel of fire, that mine own tears
> Do scald like molten lead.

(4.7.14–17; 44–48)

Lear's delusion here is that he is dead, and in hell or purgatory, and that Cordelia is one of the blessed spirits from heaven. He understands enough to know that his suffering is self-inflicted – "mine own tears do scald"; and he believes he is separated, by his own error, from Cordelia by a gulf such as that separating hell from heaven.

She appears, however, as his deliverer, as the one who will redeem him from torment. But she comes to him in a very Christian reversal, as a servant, a subject, his daughter, and she asks for his blessing in the highly charged word "benediction":

Cord. O, look upon me, sir,
And hold your hands in benediction o'er me…

(4.7.57–58)

He tries to kneel to her, since he should be the one asking forgiveness. "No, sir," she says, "you must not kneel." And in the following speech, a speech that lies at the heart of the play, Lear shows that he has found in his misfortune self-knowledge, and a simplicity of language that enables him to communicate with himself and with others as he never could before.

Pray, do not mock me.
I am a very foolish fond old man,
Fourscore and upward, not an hour more nor less;
And, to deal plainly,
I fear I am not in my perfect mind.
Methinks I should know you, and know this man;
Yet I am doubtful; for I am mainly ignorant
What place this is; and all the skill I have
Remembers not these garments; nor I know not
Where I did lodge last night. Do not laugh at me;
For, as I am a man, I think this lady
To be my child Cordelia.

(4.7.60–71)

Here lies the truth Lear has discovered: he is just an old man, and Cordelia, the lady, is his child. He knows himself to be old, frail, confused. He knows he has done his daughter wrong, and he is sorry for it. In Wilson Knight's terms, he has gained a deeper insight into both himself and the nature of the universe.

Here, then, we have forgiveness and reconciliation, understanding of the self and others; pity, sympathy, healing, and trust. And here the play must have raised expectations among its first audiences that the drama would play out towards the familiar happy ending: an expectation that must have terminated in a most bitter and cruel disappointment. After Cordelia's forces lose the battle and they are captured, Lear himself persists in the illusion that an alternative happy ending is available to them; that they will be able simply to contract out of history and make a separate peace. He envisages this solution for himself and Cordelia as a combination of imprisonment and religious sequestration:

> No, no, no, no! Come, let's away to prison.
> We two alone will sing like birds i' the cage:
> When thou dost ask me blessing, I'll kneel down,
> And ask of thee forgiveness... So we'll live...
> And take upon's the mystery of things,
> As if we were God's spies; and we'll wear out,
> In a walled prison, packs and sects of great ones,
> That ebb and flow by the moon...
> Upon such sacrifices, my Cordelia,
> The gods themselves throw incense.

(5.3.8–21)

Here Lear conceives a possible life for them as anchorites or religious hermits, a life structured around ritual and prayer and the exchange of blessing and forgiveness, which will lead the penitent into a deeper understanding of "the mystery of things". Inducted into this secret knowledge, he and Cordelia will operate as "God's spies", as double agents poised between the two worlds of heaven and earth, observing the world only to transmit the information to God. Cordelia's sacrifice – her joining her father in defeat rather than saving herself – is an act that earns divine approval, just as in the Gospels the Father is "well pleased" with the sacrifice of the Son. Lear's linking of sacrifice and incense echoes the psalter: "Let my prayer be directed in thy sight *as* incense, *and* the lifting up of mine hands as an evening sacrifice" (Psalm 141:2).

§

The death of Cordelia is the point in the play where tragedy rules supreme, and all hopes and fantasies of victory, restoration, rescue, and liberation are absolutely dashed. Edmund has previously given the order for her to be hung in her cell, and even though he himself is fatally wounded by his brother Edgar, he delays revealing this fact long enough for the order to be implemented. Lear enters the stage with Cordelia dead in his arms.

> She's gone forever!
> I know when one is dead, and when one lives;
> She's dead as earth. Lend me a looking glass;
> If that her breath will mist or stain the stone,
> Why then, she lives.

(5.3.257–61)

The distinction between life and death, the living and the dead, is here proposed as absolute: Cordelia is "dead as earth". Yet having pronounced her dead, Lear looks for signs of life, for the faintest traces of breath, invisible and inaudible, that yet may mist the mirror, "stain the stone". If it be so, "she lives".

> Thoul't come no more,
> Never, never, never, never, never!
> Do you see this? Look on her, look, her lips,
> Look there, look there! *Dies.*

(5.3.306–309)

What does Lear see in Cordelia's lips? The second speech repeats exactly the same paradox: "thou'lt come no more"; yet some motion about her lips, some stirring of breath or speech, seems to imply vitality.

Is Cordelia already dead, and the evidence of life merely the delusion of a mad old king, himself on the point of extinction? Or is she still barely alive, her actual death perhaps coinciding with that of her father? If we were looking for a reliable clinical diagnosis we would not entrust it to a mad old man, and the silence and inactivity of Edgar and Albany and Kent, who make no move to resuscitate her, seem to tell their own story. Lear's desire for Cordelia to survive, his yearning ache for a romance resolution to the tragedy, is possibly all that creates these imaginary vital signs. At the beginning of the play Lear looked to Cordelia's lips to speak a public declaration of love. But he did not listen, either to her speech or her silence; he was unable to grasp that Cordelia's lips would inevitably speak a different language. Now it is too late.

But of course "life", within the symbolic language of the drama, may mean something different from a pulse, respiration, continuing cerebral activity. What Lear feels from Cordelia's dead lips may be a breath that mists no mirror, a quickening spirit that transcends mortality, a sign of life everlasting. For many critics the language of the play's closure overtly hints at redemptive, sacrificial, Christian meanings.

> This feather stirs; she lives! If it be so,
> It is a chance which does redeem all sorrows
> That ever I have felt.

(3.5.264–66)

The feather does not stir, and yet she lives, "a soul in bliss". In an agnostic or atheist reading this is the delusion of an old man desperate to keep his dead daughter alive. In a Christian reading, assured that Cordelia's sacrificial death, like the death of Christ, has the power to "redeem all sorrows", Lear may die in sure and certain hope of the resurrection to eternal life. This, finally, may be the happy ending that is continually trying to get out of this bleak and nihilistic tragedy.

What are the interpretive options open to us in reading *King Lear*? Since the play is set in a pagan world, it is possible to argue that this Christian writer was simply portraying objectively a non-Christian society, as he clearly did in his Roman plays. On the other hand, as many modern critics have proposed, Shakespeare might have found in this pagan world a correlative of his own unbelief, producing an atheist tragedy in which the pre-Christian gods are merely metaphors for the cruelty and indifference of an empty universe.

I want to suggest another interpretation altogether: that the play could be seen as reflecting the form of Christianity to which Shakespeare was in later life becoming increasingly drawn – Calvinism. Is this so surprising? In 1604, shortly before *King Lear* appeared, Shakespeare was living with Calvinists, the Huguenot Mountjoys. He was making frequent use of the Geneva Bible, and the Calvinist-influenced *Book of Common Prayer*. As a member of the King's Men, he was a servant of James I, a monarch who had been brought up in the Calvinist Church of Scotland, and before whom *King Lear* was performed, as stated on the title page of the 1608 edition: "played before the King's Majesty at Whitehall upon St. Stephen's night in Christmas Holidays by His Majesty's Servants". For the sources of *King Lear* he drew on the anti-Catholic polemical work of Samuel Harsnett. *King Lear* has hardly ever in the past been located by critics into this Calvinist context, but it would in fact be highly unlikely that Shakespeare could fail to be influenced by it. All the evidence points in that direction. With its portrayal of the "total depravity" of mankind, its explicit concern with the incomprehensibility of the divine will and the apparent arbitrariness of election, and its investment in the paradox of a merciful God who can yet also appear cruel and indifferent, *King Lear* should perhaps be repositioned as the greatest work of Calvinist literature.

CHAPTER TEN

"THE HAND OF GOD":
THE TEMPEST AND
THE WINTER'S TALE

*Suppose a man falls among thieves, or wild beasts; is shipwrecked
at sea by a sudden gale; is killed by a falling house or tree. Suppose
another man wandering through the desert finds help in his straits;
having been tossed by the waves, reaches harbour; miraculously
escapes death by a finger's breadth. Carnal reason ascribes all such
happenings, whether prosperous or adverse, to fortune. But anyone
who has been taught by Christ's lips that all the hairs of his head
are numbered [Matt. 10:30] will look farther afield for a cause,
and will consider that all events are governed by God's secret plan.*

(John Calvin, *Institutes of the Christian Religion*, 1.16.2)

This is not a commentary on Shakespeare's late plays, but
a passage from John Calvin's *Institutes* sub-titled "There is no
such thing as fortune or chance". As part of his argument
(discussed previously in relation to *Hamlet*) that all actions and
events, however random and arbitrary they may appear, do not
happen by chance but by the workings of divine providence,
Calvin lists exactly the kinds of circumstance – shipwrecks,
narrow escapes, fatal accidents, falling prey to wild beasts – that
characterize Shakespeare's romances. Strange, miraculous,

incredible they may appear to be, but they are nonetheless the properties of God's absolute control of the world and of all human action, both of which are invariably "governed by a new, a *special, providence* of God". Calvin again refers to the passage in Matthew, discussed above, which Hamlet quotes together with Calvin's own coinage: "There is a *special providence* in the fall of a sparrow" (my italics).

Calvin here is borrowing ideas on providence and free will from St Augustine, with whom he also shares maritime metaphors, re-applied from the New Testament. "I was tossed about with every wind," says Augustine in the *Confessions*, "but yet was steered by thee, though very secretly." Drawing on the same biblical sources, Calvin writes: "He commands and raises the stormy wind which lifts on high the waves of the sea… then he causes the storm to become calm, so that the waves cease." Left to their own devices, subject to the vagaries of wind and weather, human beings would drift helplessly, or founder on the rocks, or sink without trace. Only the power of God, the same power manifested in miracles such as Christ's calming of the storm in the Gospels, can guide the little human craft safely to harbour, deliver the drowning man from the waves, rescue the marooned. Nothing is accidental: everything demonstrates the rule of a benevolent providence.

In his *On the Bondage of the Will* (1525) Luther argued, "God has taken my salvation out of the control of my own will, and put it under the control of His." Calvin doubted that human beings could really choose meaningfully at all. The fall destroyed Adam's capacity for free choice, leaving him "sunk down into spiritual destruction". Aristotle was wrong to claim that "the mind is moved by choice", and by this error he was "seeking in a ruin for a building". In Calvin's soteriology, free will is replaced by the free gift of divine grace, which guides the fallen souls of the elect "through the secret energy of the spirit".

Many scholars have shown that Shakespeare's late romances revisit the scenes of his tragedies, and reproduce them as comedy. These plays abound in potentially tragic misunderstandings and gripping near-misses that somehow, by apparently miraculous accident, produce benevolent results – family reunions, clarified misunderstandings, marriages, and reconciliations. In *Othello* and *Macbeth* paranoid jealousy and regicidal ambition have their tragic consequences; in *The Winter's Tale* and *The Tempest* the same passions are subjected to inexplicable reversals of fortune that produce comic and romantic solutions. The source of these reversals is explicitly named in both plays as "grace". In the tragedies human beings make their own choices, with disastrous and destructive results. In the late plays other humans make exactly the same choices, but before tragedy befalls them their actions are countermanded, and their freedom negated, by the secret workings of providence, operating through divine grace. I will argue that in his late plays Shakespeare demonstrably commits to the Calvinist scheme of salvation.

§

The plot of *The Tempest* is in itself predicated on "strange accident". It opens with the sorcerer Prospero, who inhabits a desert island together with his daughter Miranda, the brutish indigenous Caliban, and the spirit Ariel. Formerly the duke of Milan, Prospero was usurped and exiled by his wicked brother Antonio, in league with the duke of Naples, Alonso. Both men, together with family and courtiers from Milan and Naples, happen to be on board a ship that passes the island, and Prospero, expert in the necromantic arts, seizes the opportunity of bringing them within his power. It is he who engineers the storm and shipwreck that bring the rest of the cast safely to shore, thus discharging the god-like function of raising and quelling storms. "By accident most strange," he explains to Miranda, "bountiful Fortune,/Now my dear lady, hath mine enemies/ Brought to this shore" (1.2.179–81). Prospero uses his magic to punish and torment the sinners until they begin to repent of their crimes and come within range of forgiveness. Here is the message Prospero sends to Alonso and the two Neapolitans, Sebastian and Francisco, who have been plotting to murder him, bringing them all into the orbit of a common guilt:

> You are three men of sin, whom destiny –
> That hath to instrument this lower world
> And what is in't – the never-surfeited sea
> Hath caused to belch up you, and on this island
> Where man doth not inhabit, you 'mongst men
> Being most unfit to live. I have made you mad…
> I and my fellows
> Are ministers of Fate… you three
> From Milan did supplant good Prospero;
> Exposed unto the sea, which hath requit it,
> Him and his innocent child; for which foul deed,
> The powers, delaying not forgetting, have
> Incensed the seas and shores, yea, all the creatures,
> Against your peace.

(3.3.53–58; 60–61; 69–75)

The carrier of this message, and the instrument by which Prospero achieves his results, is his servant, the spirit Ariel. Ariel rescues the innocent and guilty alike, including the usurping Antonio, Alonso, Sebastian, and Francisco. Collectively these characters are designated by the play as "men of sin", steeped in committed or conceived criminality. The action of the play however brings them to ultimate repentance and forgiveness.

> All three of them are desperate. Their great guilt,
> Like poison given to work a great time after,
> Now 'gins to bite the spirits.

(3.3.104–106)

The characters are obliged to make public confession of their guilt, and to profess their purpose of amendment, their determination to live "clear lives" in the future. "Thy dukedom I resign," says Alonso, "and do entreat/Thou pardon me my wrongs" (5.1.120–21). The power that has brought them to this condition of repentance and amendment is explicitly named as "grace". "I'll be wise hereafter," says Caliban, guilty of an attempt on Prospero's life, "And seek for grace" (5.1.298–99); while Prospero himself refers to the "sovereign aid" of "soft grace".

Ariel is the symbolic personification of grace. He is associated with the "holy" (3.3.94) and with "grace" (3.3.84). Ariel mediates between the magician and his subjects, in much the same way as the Holy Spirit mediates between God and humanity. Twice in the play he is called a "comforter" (2.1.192; 5.1.57), the name given to the Holy Spirit in John 14:26. In the opening tempest he assumes the same form as the Holy Spirit when it descends with a "mighty wind" and "tongues, like fire" on the disciples in the Acts of the Apostles (Acts 2:2–3).

> I boarded the King's ship. Now on the beak,
> Now in the waste, the deck, in every cabin,
> I flamed amazement. Sometime I'd divide,
> And burn in many places; on the topmast,
> The yards, and bowsprit, would I flame distinctly;
> Then meet and join. Jove's lightning, the precursors
> O'th' dreadful thunderclaps, more momentary
> And sight-outrunning were not. The fire and cracks

Of sulphurous roaring the most mighty Neptune
Seem to besiege, and make his bold waves tremble,
Yea, his dread trident shake.

(1.2.196–206)

The Spirit, says Calvin, "is justly called 'fire'" (Luke 3:16). Thus Ariel visits sinners with the "initiating grace" that in Calvin's doctrine is the prerequisite of repentance: "Both repentance and forgiveness of sins – that is, newness of life and free reconciliation – are conferred on us by Christ" (*Institutes*, 3.3.1). Ariel also prompts Prospero towards forgiveness of those who have wronged him, in sentiments that recall *Measure for Measure*: "if you now beheld them, your affections/Would become tender" (5.1.18–19).

Some of Shakespeare's tragic heroes – Macbeth, Othello, Hamlet – listen to something outside themselves that prompts them toward a certain course of action: the witches, or the tempter Iago, or the ghost. But the psychological processes that drive them towards a tragic end happen within themselves, and are charted by Shakespeare with astonishing verisimilitude. These men make their own fate, as does Lear, who needs no external stimulus – it is he, and he alone, who opens the mental gate that lets his folly in and his dear judgment out. In the late romances these inner drivers are either not there at all, or they are negated by the operation of external powers. But this is not because the romances are inferior to the tragedies in their portrayals of "character". Prospero brings sinners, including himself, into the environment of repentance and forgiveness by inflicting magical forces upon them. The opportunity of repentance does not come from within, but is applied externally (as Calvin says of grace, "conferred on us"), afforded solely by providence.

§

Othello (1603) and *The Winter's Tale* (1611) both begin with exactly the same psychological crisis: a husband plunged into desperate and murderous jealousy by fantasies of his wife's adultery:

> *Othello.* She's gone. I am abused, and my relief
> Must be to loathe her. O curse of marriage,
> That we can call these delicate creatures ours
> And not their appetites! I had rather be a toad
> And live upon the vapour of a dungeon,
> Than keep a corner in the thing I love
> For others' uses. Yet 'tis the plague of great ones;
> Prerogatived are they less than the base.
> 'Tis destiny unshunnable, like death.
> Even then this forked plague is fated to us
> When we do quicken.

(*Othello*: 3.3.271–81)

> *Leontes.* Gone already.
> Inch-thick, knee-deep, o'er head and ears a forked one! –
> Go play, boy, play. Thy mother plays, and I
> Play too, but so disgraced a part, whose issue
> Will hiss me to my grave. Contempt and clamour
> Will be my knell… Physic for't there's none.
> It is a bawdy planet, that will strike
> Where 'tis predominant…

(*The Winter's Tale*: 1.2.185–91; 201–203)

It is exactly the same passion, expressed in the same form: the fetid imagination that broods on perverse fantasies of sexual betrayal; the horror of sharing an intimate possession with strangers; the fear that female infidelity is a universal condition afflicting all men alike; and the sense of an irrevocable decision that cannot be revoked: "She's gone"; "Gone already."

But there is a huge difference between the tragedy and the romance. Othello reaches this position after a long and slow process of temptation by the demonic Iago; Leontes in *The Winter's Tale* collapses into the torment of jealousy with irrational suddenness and precipitation. Othello reasons with Iago, resists his arguments, doubts his evidence, only very gradually assents to his suspicions, and in a fatal error chooses to doubt Desdemona's honesty; Leontes switches in a rapid and dizzying reversal from affection to paranoid hatred, one moment appreciating his wife's courteous behaviour, the next seeing it as proof of covert lechery: "Too hot, too hot!" The tragedy presents character as development, evolution, drawn with astounding dramatic skill and horrifying psychological verisimilitude; the romance displays passion as an ungovernable instinct that springs fully formed from the diseased imagination of sinful humanity. Shakespeare has shifted his emphasis from the study of tragic choice, what the Greeks called "*hamartia*" or "fatal flaw", to an exploration of irrational passion as a calamity that seems almost accidental, certainly inexplicable. The results of the same passion in the tragedy and the romance can be similar – Othello kills his wife; Leontes' son Mamillius perishes – but in the romance some higher power seems to intervene in the tragic process, literally reversing its logic – Desdemona dies, but Leontes' wife Hermione lives; Othello has no recourse but to kill himself, while Leontes repents and is reunited with his estranged wife and his abandoned daughter (named by others Perdita, the lost one).

Leontes is if anything far more guilty than Othello in terms of the crimes he almost commits, which include the murder of his friend Polixenes as well as the rejection of his wife and the abandonment of their daughter. Where Othello pays the ultimate price, Leontes' crimes do not generate a tragic denouement. As in *The Tempest*, the power that impels such providential reversals is explicitly named as "grace". Hermione's alleged guilt is referred to the Delphic Oracle: "Gracious be the issue!" It is a word much used by the innocent and wronged Hermione, who calls both her marriage and her imprisonment examples of "grace". Hermione never loses her conviction that providence will eventually champion her cause and justify her:

> if powers divine
> Behold our human actions – as they do –
> I doubt not then but innocence shall make
> False accusation blush...

(3.2.26–29)

Leontes' repentance does not have to wait on such revelations, but begins in the trial scene, as suddenly as did his jealousy, with the news that his son has died: "I have too much believed mine own suspicion..." (3.2.149).

But Leontes' relenting comes too late for the immediate and unproblematical restoration he envisages and hopes for:

> I'll reconcile me to Polixenes,
> New woo my queen, recall the good Camillo,
> Whom I proclaim a man of truth, of mercy...

(3.2.153–55)

Hermione, however, has disappeared, rescued by the faithful Paulina and hidden, where she will remain for sixteen years, during which Leontes thinks her dead as a direct consequence of his own sins. In the course of this long interlude Leontes is effectively handed over to the moral care of Paulina, whose name links her to St Paul, and whose continual remonstrations inevitably recall the exhortations to the churches in the Pauline epistles. Though others try to persuade Leontes he has done enough to satisfy the requirements of penitence and should feel absolved, Paulina continues to insist that since the effect of Leontes' primary sin, the (supposed) death of Hermione, remains perpetually irrevocable, he cannot expect to move from repentance to absolution:

> *Cleomones.* Sir, you have done enough, and have performed
> A saint-like sorrow. No fault could you make
> Which you have not redeemed, indeed, paid down
> More penitence than done trespass. At the last,
> Do as the heavens have done, forget your evil.
> With them, forgive yourself.
> *Leontes.* Whilst I remember
> Her and her virtues, I cannot forget
> My blemishes in them, and so still think of
> The wrong I did myself, which was so much,
> That heirless it hath made my kingdom, and
> Destroyed the sweet'st companion that e'er man
> Bred his hopes out of. True?
> *Paulina.* Too true, my lord.
> If one by one you wedded all the world,
> Or from the all that are took something good
> To make a perfect woman, she you killed
> Would be unparalleled.

(5.1.1–16)

By focusing Leontes' sin on the missing body of his wife, Paulina simultaneously presses home his remorse and prepares the way for the restoration of that same body through the device of the "living statue". One of Othello's final fantasies is to imagine Desdemona as fixed in "monumental alabaster", pure and incorruptible, for him infinitely preferable to the living, breathing, corruptible woman. In *The Winter's Tale* Hermione literally becomes such a statue, that figures forth her innocence, and then appears to come to life in a simulated resurrection. Both mother and father are then reunited with their lost daughter. The dead rise; the lost are found. These biblical tropes are not advanced as real probabilities, but as religious archetypes. In the context of a realistic portrayal of human behaviour, they are incredible and absurd. But in the context of Christian doctrine as interpreted by Calvin, they are exactly what we should expect of the world:

> *since the order, reason, end and necessity of those things which happen for the most part lie hidden in God's purpose, and are not apprehended by human opinion, those things, which it is certain take place by God's will, are in a sense fortuitous… what for us seems a contingency, faith recognizes to have been a secret impulse from God.*

(*Institutes*, 1.6 and 1.9)

CONCLUSION

Shakespeare was a Protestant, who would have written quite differently if the Reformation had never occurred.

To recapitulate, the Reformation was an immensely significant series of changes in European religion, which effected a radical break with the past, and shaped the pattern of Christianity in the future. As with all such momentous changes, historians have disagreed fundamentally about how and why it happened, and what it meant. In a cultural environment where the intelligentsia is overwhelmingly Protestant (like mid-Victorian Britain), then the Reformation was likely to be interpreted as a great leap forward in human history, a theological and ecclesiastical revolution parallel to the Renaissance. The Reformation brought religious liberty, intellectual freedom and national sovereignty, and ushered in the modern world. The reign of Elizabeth I was celebrated by such "Whig" history (historiography that sees the past as leading inevitably to greater freedom and enlightenment, culminating in the modern democratic state with its constitutional monarchy) as a Protestant Golden Age, in which an independent British nation formed itself around a common Protestant religion, a common national language, and a successful monarchy. The achievement of Shakespeare and all the other great writers of the English Renaissance flourished in this Protestant environment, and under the patronage of a Protestant monarchy and nobility.

The "Whig" view of history was identified and challenged particularly after the First World War, when it became harder to see the world as continually improving. Catholic historians had been offering quite different views of the Reformation ever since the sixteenth century. The first such work was Nicholas Sanders's *Rise and Growth of the Anglican Schism* (1585), and great modern historians such as Eammon Duffy have provided sustained critiques of the earlier Protestant consensus. In this paradigm, the Reformation can be seen as an unfortunate and even unnecessary deviation in the history of the church. "Top-down" religious revolutions do not really change peoples' beliefs, though they can force conformity. In Duffy's view large numbers of English people remained Roman Catholic at heart for many years. This thesis helps to explain why in later centuries the Anglican Church recovered much of its pre-Reformation Catholic heritage in the form of a hybrid and synthesized "Anglo-Catholicism".

The Reformation can be seen as a movement of ruthless dogmatism that dismantled entire structures of community, and destroyed a precious cultural inheritance, leaving the Christian believer alone in a universe ruled by an inscrutable and potentially terrifying God. It can even be seen as one source of modern fundamentalism. But the Reformation can also be understood as a narrative of spiritual liberation, freeing the minds of the people from superstition. It can be seen as a fundamentalist reform, recovering the pure wellspring of Christian belief that had been polluted by Catholic tradition. Believers given direct access to the Holy Scriptures, through vernacular translation, were able to discover their own version of God, unmediated by clerical authority. Secular liberals can easily relate to this narrative: the Reformation can be seen as the birth of modern individualism, capitalism, democracy. And this is the Reformation that gave birth to Shakespeare.

§

What role did religion play in Shakespeare's own personal life? If we set aside the idea that the plays and poems are autobiographical, the Shakespeare biography consists entirely of historical records. Everything we can know about the faith of William Shakespeare lies in the historical evidence about his life, and in his works, which are likely to omit what biography really wants most of all to know, the interior life, the secrets of the private man: how he felt, whom he loved, what he believed. Biographical data can tell us with certainty about Shakespeare's public performance of religion, as a conforming member of the Church of England; and can produce circumstantial evidence suggesting he might have been a Catholic. The plays are written by a Christian who could safely assume the same faith on the part of his audience, but mapping the religious sentiments to be found in them onto the poet's personal belief system is a more difficult, though not (as I have demonstrated) impossible, operation.

More recent scholarship and criticism have begun to acknowledge that religion played a vital role in early modern culture, not least in the work of Shakespeare. But there is no agreement about what Shakespeare's faith actually was. Some contemporary scholars have characterized Shakespeare as a "parish Anglican", for whom religion was a matter of habit, conventional custom, and social practice, rather than earnest personal struggle. I have argued on the contrary that Shakespeare was a loyal and faithful servant of the Church of England, who attended its services, structured his life around its rituals, absorbed and reproduced its liturgies, and grew increasingly attached to its doctrines. He was indeed an "Anglican" (before the word was invented), with a natural affection for the Catholic roots of the church, who had moved by the end of his life towards the more Protestant position articulated in his will and expressed in the religious perspectives active in his later plays.

§

In discussing Shakespeare's own play about the Reformation, *Henry VIII*, I have offered a reading which makes the play sound almost like Protestant propaganda, dependent on the work of Tudor historians such as Holinshed, Halle, and Foxe, who promoted the Tudor dynasty and the Henrician Reformation in terms of Calvinist providentialism as the divinely ordained destiny of England. And it is true that the play closely follows the ideology of these Protestant historiographers. The villain of the piece is Cardinal Wolsey, and King Henry the hero; the papacy and the Catholic Church are shown in an unfavourable light, while the emergent Protestant elite represented by Anne Boleyn, Thomas Cranmer (the Boleyn family chaplain), and Thomas Cromwell are hailed as the saviours of the kingdom. The play shows the destabilizing effects of Cardinal Wolsey's ambition and of his divided allegiance, which prefers the pope to the king, and comes to rest on the vision of a kingdom united in both loyalty and faith under a Protestant sovereign.

It would also be true to say that this sounds like an oversimplification, and not what one would expect from a Shakespeare play. Those who see the play as relatively simplistic in its representation of history are more likely to attribute this feature to the possible collaborative context of its production. If Shakespeare was not fully in charge of the play – if for example John Fletcher wrote substantial parts of it – that might explain why it seems more polemical and dogmatic than most of his historical dramas. These latter, as we have seen when considering *Richard II* and *Henry V*, prefer to draw on historical sources with conflicting ideologies, and use them to produce dramatic tension and diversity of interpretation. Those critics who see the play as genuinely Shakespearean tend to emphasize the complexities and ambiguities of the play. Wolsey, for example, is a fully realized tragic figure, whose virtues are described along with his vices, not a one-dimensional pantomime villain.

After his fall from favour Catherine and a servant alternately list Wolsey's vices and virtues (4.2.31–68). The source is a passage of Holinshed in which the historian merges both, rendering a complex portrait of Wolsey as a great man fatally flawed. Shakespeare has carefully disaggregated the polarized characteristics and divided them between two characters in the play. Catherine of Aragon is treated very sympathetically in the play, and given substantial dramatic depth as a figure of tragic pathos, and Anne Boleyn is perhaps not as "saint-like" as Tudor propaganda would wish to see her. But none of this nuance can alter the fact that the play is dominated by a strong and affirmative Protestantism.

§

Shakespeare's earlier history plays are less explicit in terms of their confessional position. Nonetheless I have been able to show that in the figures of Richard II and Henry V, Shakespeare offered a distinction and contrast between a broadly Catholic and an intensively Protestant way of being a ruler. The first perceives authority as sacral, deriving unconditionally from divine sanction, directly transmitted through the levels of a hierarchical society. The second understands power as emerging and evolving contingently from below, and as dependent on a recognition of the difference between language and reality, or between the signifier and its referent. This distinction parallels the religious controversies of the day over the meanings of signification, especially in the Eucharist – controversies that were embodied particularly in *The Book of Common Prayer.*

Of course this distinction is anachronistic, since the period 1399–1415 pre-dates the Reformation, and both these monarchs knew nothing other than the mediaeval Catholic Church of Rome. Indeed Henry V was a notorious persecutor of the proto-Protestant Lollard movement. Nor does it align with the kinds of identification actually made in Shakespeare's day, when sixteenth-century leaders were compared with their counterparts of the past: at the time of the Essex rebellion Protestant Elizabeth compared herself to Catholic Richard II. The interactions between present and past were notoriously complex. Shakespeare was always careful to construct accurate and believable portrayals of historic societies, so the world of these plays is always recognizably that of the fifteenth century: for example, at the beginning of *Henry V* the king presents himself as politically dependent on the papal-appointed clergy, the bishops. But Shakespeare was also a man of his time, conscious that his audience wanted to view the present in the past, hence it soon becomes clear that the fictional Henry V, like the real Henry VIII, has in fact thoroughly subjugated the authority of the church to that of the crown, and is already a national sovereign like Elizabeth I. The political order of the play is an anachronistically post-Reformation polity. In these historical dramas the past is configured partly in terms derived from the present; and the past in turn tends to break free from its historical containment to pose urgent questions to Shakespeare's own world.

I have argued that Shakespeare's contrast between Richard II and Henry V is deliberately constructed to echo key theological debates of the Reformation. Like the Roman Catholic Church (as depicted by the reformers), Richard mistakes mere symbols for realities, and is "in bondage to the figure". Henry on the other hand understands that power is not inherent in the symbols that represent it, and that the person of the king is dissociable from his office. This semiotic awareness enables him to manipulate signs in order to exploit the realities of power. Richard's literal and absolutist perspective convinces him that the king can do no wrong; whereas Henry knows that the king is accountable to external standards, and will be judged and measured by them.

Richard encounters his own mortality as a shocking revelation that comes to him only in despair, and enables him to do nothing other than surrender. Henry's Protestant knowledge of human frailty and culpability becomes a condition of his power.

§

Measure for Measure is a play that shows an active interest in matters of religion, and an engagement in matters of doctrinal controversy. Shakespeare draws on the resources of the Bible, *The Book of Common Prayer*, and contemporary theological debate to construct a play in which religion counts – it can indeed be a matter of life and death. Some critics have argued that the play is inflected towards a Catholic orthodoxy, since it presents Angelo's fragile sanctity as an indictment of Puritanism, and validates the duke's Catholic persona as a force for good. In this context traditional Catholic confession is seen as a vital circulation of what would otherwise be inaccessible layers of truth, concealed within the minds and hearts of the characters. The duke as confessor is able to tap into this enclosed domain of privacy and draw its multifarious threads together into a web of knowledge that enables him to apportion justice and achieve social equilibrium.

But confession in *Measure for Measure* is not sealed and secret, and the duke is not a priest but a secular ruler who arrogates spiritual authority, like Henry VIII or James I. Auricular confession haunts the play, but it is shown in the end to be inadequate as a means of attaining religious and social harmony. In the last act the duke stages a different kind of confession, a general public admission of "natural guiltiness". Even those characters who are not specifically guilty are obliged to join in the universal self-condemnation, as in the general confession and absolution from *The Book of Common Prayer*:

Almighty God… we acknowledge and bewail our manifold sins and wickedness… have mercy upon us… forgive us all that is past…

¶ *Then shall the priest… stand up, and turning himself to the people, shall say thus.*

Almighty God, our heavenly father, who of his great mercy hath promised forgiveness of sins, to all them, which with hearty repentance and true faith turn to him: have mercy upon you, pardon and deliver you from all your sins, confirm and strengthen you in all goodness, and bring you to everlasting life; through Jesus Christ our Lord. Amen.

§

The Merchant of Venice (clearly derivative of Marlowe's *The Jew of Malta*) is unusual in Shakespeare's work in that it concerns a conflict between Christianity and another world faith, Judaism. The play is set in Venice, known to English intellectuals as a Catholic state that was nonetheless anti-papal and relatively tolerant, certainly more congenial to the many English travellers who visited and even lived there than the papal headquarters of Rome. Here Shakespeare is less interested in the differences between Catholic and Protestant positions, and more interested in affirming the values of Christianity against those of the parent religion from which it derived.

Both Shakespeare's Venetian plays present a very early manifestation of Venice as a fragile and vulnerable construction, as likely to disappear into the waters of the lagoon as to endure unchanged for eternity. A city that could conceivably sink beneath the waves presents a paradigm of social solubility. If every member of Venetian society recognizes this common condition, this proximity of dissolution, co-existence remains possible. If all parties recognize that in Venice Christians, Jews, and Moors shared a common difference, then co-existence could be possible, even on the basis of mutual dislike. If differences are promoted by any party to the point of social fracture, the society is in danger of collapse, and is obliged to re-establish unity by force. This restitution of hegemony will surely look like the assertion of a power that was always there, the existence of which calls into question its ideals of tolerance and inclusiveness and respect for diversity. Surely these ideals were never genuine if the state always retained the power to over-ride them? Shakespeare's Venetian plays however show a different aspect to that process of imposing power, which is always invoked in the last instance as the only effective means of preserving the tolerance and inclusiveness and diversity that inevitably challenge it. Meanwhile the vision of another possibility, one in which all peoples acknowledge the common authority that preserves their differences, shines faintly but truly through the darkness of tragedy and tragicomedy. "How far that little candle throws his beams!" (5.1.89).

§

Hamlet begins as a play about destiny, and ends as a play about providence. Prior to the appearance of the ghost, Hamlet seems to have no motivation, no plan for the future, and no ambition. He is overwhelmed by the grief of bereavement, by hatred and suspicion of his uncle, and by disgust towards his mother; but his only willed course of action is to leave the court and return to university in Wittenberg. He has no conception of himself as a revenger, or a hero, or a man of destiny.

The ghost's visitation changes all this. By confirming Claudius's guilt, alerting Hamlet to his father's posthumous suffering, and commanding him to take revenge, the ghost sets Hamlet on a path that leads him inevitably to the final fatal denouement in which he kills the king, but only at the price of his own and his mother's death. Hamlet now has a destiny, though it is not one he welcomes. As Marcellus observes, "Something is rotten in the state of Denmark", and it falls to Hamlet to find and root it out:

> O cursed spite!
> That ever I was born to set it right!

(1.5.189–90)

There is something pessimistic about this reluctant hero accepting his destiny that suggests both the fatalism of Scandinavian paganism, and classical philosophies such as Stoicism. Inside the drama Hamlet's destiny is also continually defined as a specific theatrical role, that of the revenge hero, which has to be played out within a predetermined tragic pattern. Hamlet often describes himself as trapped inside a narrative that evolves by itself, and takes him with it: he is "bounded in a nutshell", and devoid of free will. By the end of the play however Hamlet has reached an understanding of the destiny that has been prepared for him, and names it "providence". He accepts it, co-operates with it, and disciplines his actions to ensure its unimpeded operation. His destiny turns out to be something he was indeed born for, and is explicitly defined as nothing less than John Calvin's doctrine of predestination.

§

Those who in the 1960s began to attack the predominantly religious view of Shakespeare's plays focused particularly on *King Lear*. In doing so they tended to assume that a Christian universe should be one that delivers redemption, as for example through the "happy ending" evident in the legendary histories and romances; should manifest the ubiquitous presence of a universally merciful God; and should demonstrate a "sure and certain hope" in salvation. The fact that the play manifestly fails to deliver on all these points – the happy ending is cruelly controverted; the fates of the characters seem to reveal no plan of divine justice; and faith is left to be inferred from the hopes and anxieties of an old and dying man – provided a basis for reinterpreting the play as an atheist or agnostic tragedy.

But here the play was being measured against the wrong criteria. The dominant form of Christianity in the Church of England in 1605 did not see the world as unproblematically committed to redemption, did not regard God as comprehensively merciful, and saw the proper grounds of faith in anxiety and uncertainty rather than sureness of conviction. Calvin thought that the problem of whether God was merciful, and if so to whom, was "inexplicable". Faced with the spectacle of a God who might choose to save all, but instead chooses to save only some, Calvinists existed in a state of spiritual anxiety concerning the condition of their souls. Does the believer have true faith? Do we fear God in the right way? Should we even ask such questions, given that we cannot possibly know God and his intentions for us? "Involved in the mists of error," Calvin stated, "we attain not at all." In this respect Calvin was building on Luther's conviction of the incomprehensibility of God:

> *Inasmuch as He is the one true God, wholly incomprehensible*
> *and inaccessible to man's understanding, it is reasonable, indeed*
> *inevitable, that His justice should also be incomprehensible… what*
> *perversity is it on our part to worry at the justice and the judgement*
> *of the only God, and to arrogate so much to our own judgement as*
> *to presume to comprehend, judge, and evaluate God's judgement.*

(Luther, *On the Bondage of the Will*)

"With this curb," Calvin continued, "God keeps us modest… that every teacher, however excellent, may still be disposed to learn." Our failure to understand God compels us to redirect our knowledge to our own humanity, and to realize both the limitations of our own understanding and the frailty of our fallen nature. To believe otherwise would be to believe, like Shakespeare's Edmund ("in his own grace he doth exalt himself" [*King Lear* 5.3.70]), in the freedom of the human will.

> *The human mind, when blinded and darkened, is very far from being able to rise to proper knowledge of the divine will; nor can the heart, fluctuating with perpetual doubt, rest secure on such knowledge. Hence… the mind must be enlightened, and the heart confirmed, from some other quarter.*

(*Institutes*, 3.2.7)

That is, from God himself acting through the operation of grace. We cannot control or demand reassurance of faith – faith itself is a form of anxiety: "by desiring to believe they prove themselves to be true believers". Genuine faith is what Calvin paradoxically called a kind of "diffidence" about our own capacities for understanding. We can desire God's grace without being certain we have it. We are like Cordelia in *King Lear*: "But yet, alas," she laments, "stood I within his grace!" (1.1.282).

Lear's whole life, as we see it unfold in the play, begins as an anxious quest for the reassurance of love – "Which of you shall we say doth love us most?"(1.1.49) – and resolves into a soul-searching Protestant anxiety about the very nature of being: "Who is it that can tell me who I am?" (1.4.205). There seems to be so little love in the play, as compared to the quantity of evil, hatred, selfishness, and brutality, that the questing soul must needs look elsewhere for reassurance. But where? How is it possible to know if you are loved by others or by God? There can only be one possible answer: grace. Deprived of divine love, "Without our grace, our love, our benison" (1.1.266) – as Lear says to Cordelia – humanity is nothing.

§

It should come as no surprise that Shakespeare in his later plays conformed so closely to the central doctrines of Calvinism. It was after all the characteristic position of the Church of England in which he worshipped; it was the everyday form of his religious practice. Every time Shakespeare attended morning prayer, he would have spoken this confession:

> Almighty and most merciful father, we have erred and strayed from thy ways, like lost sheep we have followed too much the devises and desires of our own hearts. We have offended against thy holy laws: We have left undone those things which we ought to have done, and we have done those things which we ought not to have done, and there is no health in us.

"No health" equals Calvin's "total depravity". In the same service Shakespeare would have heard this Collect "*for Grace*", which according to the rubric "*shall never alter, but daily be stayed at Morning prayer, throughout all the year*":

> O Lord our heavenly father, almighty and everlasting God, which hast safely brought us to the beginning of this day: defend us in the same with thy mighty power, and grant that this day we fall into no sin, neither run into any kind of danger, but that all our doings may be ordered by thy governance, to do always that is righteous in thy sight: through Jesus Christ our Lord. Amen.

All human actions are determined by God's providence. Every time Shakespeare attended the service of Holy Communion he would have said this General Confession:

> Almighty God, father of our Lord Jesus Christ, maker of all things, Judge of all men, we acknowledge and bewail our manifold sins

and wickedness, which we from time to time most grievously have committed, by thought, word and deed, against thy divine Majesty, provoking most justly thy wrath and indignation against us: we do earnestly repent, and be heartily sorry for these our misdoings, the remembrance of them is grievous unto us: the burthen of them is intolerable: have mercy upon us, have mercy upon us, most merciful father, for thy son our Lord Jesus Christ's sake, forgive us all that is past, and grant that we may ever hereafter serve and please thee, in newness of life, to the honour and glory of thy name; through Jesus Christ our Lord.

And he would have received this absolution:

Almighty God, our heavenly father, who of his great mercy hath promised forgiveness of sins, to all them, which with hearty repentance and true faith turn to him: have mercy upon you, pardon and deliver you from all your sins, confirm and strengthen you in all goodness, and bring you to everlasting life; through Jesus Christ our Lord. Amen.

"Hearty repentance and true faith" are the *sine qua non* of forgiveness. We know that Shakespeare was familiar with *Certain Sermons*, the official collection of homilies appointed to be read in churches, the first of which was published by Cranmer in 1547, and the second by Bishop John Jewel in 1571. Both collections contain a Calvinist emphasis on the incapacity of humanity for free choice without the prompting of grace:

It is of the free grace and mercy of God, by the mediation of the blood of his Son Jesus Christ, without merit or deserving on our part, that our sins are forgiven us, that we are reconciled and brought again into his favour, and are made heirs of his heavenly kingdom. Grace (saith St. Augustine) belonging to God, who doth call us, and

*then hath he good works, whosoever received grace. Good works then
bring not forth grace: but are brought forth by grace.*

("An Homily of Good Works", 1563)

Human beings are "without merit or deserving"; and subject
entirely to the generosity of divine grace.

In Shakespeare's late romances grace, operating through
a combination of apparent accident and blind human action,
works to reverse the tragic errors of the characters, and to produce
comic and romantic resolutions foregrounding forgiveness and
reconciliation. Whereas in the tragedies events are driven by
characters and the choices they make, in the romances human
freedom is strictly relative to the divine plan.

*I say then, that though all things are ordered by the counsel and
certain arrangement of God, to us, however, they are fortuitous, –
not because we imagine that Fortune rules the world and mankind,
and turns all things upside down at random, (far be such a
heartless thought from every Christian breast;) but as the order,
method, end, and necessity of events, are, for the most part, hidden
in the counsel of God, though it is certain that they are produced by
the will of God, they have the appearance of being fortuitous, such
being the form under which they present themselves to us, whether
considered in their own nature, or estimated according to our
knowledge and judgement… all the changes which take place in the
world are produced by the secret agency of the hand of God.*

(*Institutes*, 1.16.9)

INDEX

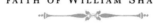